(PHOTO BY: JUDE DILLON)

About the Author

Brian Brennan is an award-winning Alberta author who specializes in books about the people and the social history of Western Canada. His most recent book, *Scoundrels and Scallywags: Characters from Alberta's Past* (Fifth House, 2002), was short-listed for the 2003 Grant MacEwan Author's Award, one of the richest literary prizes in Canada. His other books include *Alberta Originals: Stories of Albertans Who Made a Difference* and *Building a Province: 60 Alberta Lives,* both published by Fifth House Ltd. He is also the author of *Máire Bhuí Ní Laoire: A Poet of her People* (The Collins Press), which was nominated for the Irish Times Literature Prize in 2001. He has won two Western Magazine Awards and the national Hollobon Award for his journalism.

Web site: www.brian-brennan.com

Dedicated in memory
of my nineteenth
century Irish ancestor,
Máire Bhuí Ní Laoire
(Yellow Mary O'Leary),
a poet and storyteller
who lit the torch
and passed it on.

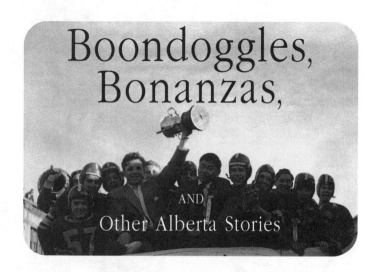

Boondoggles, Bonanzas,
AND
Other Alberta Stories

Brian Brennan

Brian Brennan (signature)

**FIFTH
HOUSE**

Cover design by John Luckhurst / GDL
Interior design by Kathy Aldous-Schleindl
Front cover photograph San Diego Historical Society 81-9775
Front cover background photograph J. David Andrews / Masterfile
Edited / copyedited by Meaghan Craven
Proofread by Alex Frazer-Harrison
Scans by St. Solo Computer Graphics

The publisher gratefully acknowledges
the support of The Canada Council
for the Arts and the Department
of Canadian Heritage.

THE CANADA COUNCIL | LE CONSEIL DES ARTS
FOR THE ARTS | DU CANADA
SINCE 1957 | DEPUIS 1957

We acknowledge the financial support of the Government of Canada through the Book Publishing Industry Development Program (BPIDP) for our publishing activities.

Printed in Canada by Friesens
03 04 05 06 07 / 5 4 3 2 1

First published in the United States in 2003 by
Fitzhenry & Whiteside
121 Harvard Avenue, Suite 2
Allston, MA 02134

National Library of Canada Cataloguing in Publication Data
Brennan, Brian, 1943–
    Boondoggles, bonanzas, and other Alberta stories / Brian Brennan.
    Includes index.
    ISBN 1-894004-94-9
    1. Alberta–History–Anecdotes.   2. Alberta–Biography.   I. Title.
FC3661.8.B73 2003   971.23   C2003-911218-7

Fifth House Ltd.
Fitzhenry & Whiteside
1511, 1800-4 St. SW
Calgary, Alberta T2S 2S5
1-800-387-9776
www.fitzhenry.ca

Contents

Introduction

THIS BOOK BEGAN with a proposition from my publisher, a tantalizing offer that I couldn't refuse: How would I like to write a book of stories about some of the events that have engaged the attention of Albertans over the years? No particular theme, no governing concept, no specific time frame—just a potpourri of tales that appealed to me and would also be of interest to the general public.

Of course, I jumped at the chance. What storyteller wouldn't? Here was an opportunity to roam across the wide range of Alberta history, pick out the stories that I thought should be told or retold, and write them for a new generation. I could revisit the big events that once were front-page news—such as the Frank Slide, the Leduc oil discovery, and Calgary's first Grey Cup win—and give them a new spin for a contemporary readership. With a bit of luck, I would also find other stories along the way that would turn out to be the nuggets in the muskeg—the gems that nobody had ever noticed before, just lying there waiting to be discovered.

I began the project with a series of questions to myself. How did the missionary priest Father Albert Lacombe end up becoming the president of the Canadian Pacific Railway, albeit for only one hour? Why did a group of nuns keep Father Lacombe's preserved heart under lock and key for more than seventy-five years after he died? Why did the famed French actress Sarah Bernhardt decide to perform in Edmonton and Calgary in 1913? Why did three Alberta aviators never get the credit for flying the first heavier-than-air plane in Canada? How did Rudyard Kipling become involved in Medicine Hat's domestic problems shortly after it became a city? Why was Alberta part of a top-secret Allied wartime initiative to build aircraft carriers out of ice? How did a group of single male ranchers in

1

Dorothy, Alberta, become the romantic targets of women from around the world?

I asked myself these questions as if I were an outsider, a newcomer to Alberta. While I have lived in this province for close to thirty years, and have written three previous books and countless magazine and newspaper articles on the social history of the place, I still like to approach its history as if I had just arrived here and had no idea what a Chinook was or who Ernest Manning might have been. I usually find that it helps to start with a clean slate; there are always new angles to be found or old myths to be shattered.

I encountered a few surprises as I embarked on this voyage of discovery. I was unaware, for example, that uncontrolled coal mining under Turtle Mountain, not the inherent geological instability of the mountain as is often suggested, was the most likely cause of the Frank Slide. And I didn't know that uncontrolled coal mining took place under an Edmonton residential district for more than fifteen years without any regulatory authority intervening. Why did authorities not intervene in these two cases? Because in each instance, the dictates of big business prevailed over the safety concerns of the local citizens. Coal mining was indeed big business in this province for more than fifty years, particularly in such places as Drumheller and Lethbridge, as well as in Edmonton and the Crowsnest Pass. Today, coal mined in Alberta supplies less than twelve percent of the province's energy demands. However, before petroleum products and natural gas began to proliferate in this province during the 1950s, "king coal"—as the mineral was once called—supplied more than half of what we needed for domestic heating, industrial energy, and railway locomotive fuel.

It was also a surprise for me to learn that Alberta's first oil boom occurred not in Turner Valley or Leduc—where some of the province's most spectacular discoveries have taken place—but in what is now Waterton Lakes National Park. If today's drilling technology had been available back then, the province's oil industry might have evolved in a completely different fashion. It was also a surprise to discover just how close Imperial Oil was to getting out of the oil business in Western Canada just before it hit pay dirt at Leduc in 1947.

The Leduc strike was a bonanza for Alberta. The Waterton Lakes strike seems to have been a bit of a boondoggle because the initial discovery well ran dry within a short time and the only people who ended up making money from the boom were the local ranchers who sold their properties to the oil companies. This is a recurring pattern in Alberta history. For every bonanza there seems to be a corresponding boondoggle. Medicine Hat's bonanza was the plentiful supply of natural gas in its cellar that caused Rudyard Kipling to declare that the town had "all hell for a basement." The region's boondoggle occurred when the Medicine Hat farmers decided they had to resort to desperate measures to protect themselves from drought, and a California "rainmaker" named Charles Hatfield took advantage of their vulnerability to make some money.

Another pattern to emerge from the pages of our one-hundred-year-old history is the fact that those who dare to be bold and different are the ones who often end up making their mark. Nobody—except for one or two close family members—gave Ralph Klein much of a chance when he announced he was going to run for mayor of Calgary in 1980. Yet, as he told me a few years later, he knew he was destined for a career as a public advocate of some kind when he realized he had lost his objectivity as a television news reporter. That's probably not something he would talk about today. Klein, the veteran politician, is now more guarded, rarely gives interviews, and when he does is not likely to reveal much of his inner life. But when I sat down with him in 1988 to do a magazine story about a day in the life of the mayor, he was happy to answer all the questions I put to him about his reporting habits (aggressive), his religious beliefs (ambivalent), his recreational activities (fishing), and his reading preferences (suspense novels). I kept all the notes from those interviews and when I went back to review them before writing this book, I was surprised at how candid Klein had been.

The Klein story is one of two in this book that resulted from lengthy interviews I conducted with the principals involved. The other is the remarkable story of the woman from the Evergreen Mobile Home Park, Marin Athanasopoulos, who survived the Edmonton tornado. Her graphic account of what it was like to be in the midst of the twister moved me to such an extent that I felt the most effective way to tell this story was to make ample use of her voice and words.

Interviews with the people connected with the early days of the Alberta folk festival movement and the beginnings of the Calgary Tower also helped bring those stories to life. The other stories in this book came mainly from secondary sources—books, newspapers, academic journals, magazines, and archival records.

I am indebted to my many friends who are writers and history enthusiasts, and who gave me useful story ideas when I first started talking about doing this book. They have been the advisory committee for all of my books and I will never be able to repay them for their support and generosity. I also want to thank Charlene Dobmeier, publisher at Fifth House Ltd., who first suggested this project and then gave me freedom to do it my way. Additionally, I would like to acknowledge the financial assistance of the Alberta Historical Resources Foundation, which covered some of my research expenses. And my eternal gratitude goes to the history librarians and archivists at the Glenbow Museum in Calgary, and the Calgary Public Library, who always have the answers to my questions.

Brian Brennan
June 2003

A Gold Mine
in the Rockies—1870

Senator Dan Riley, chronicler of the Lost Lemon Mine
saga: "It's a good story. And why ruin a good story?"

HE FOUND THE gold and then lost it. Was it ever really there? The fable of Alberta's Lost Lemon Mine falls into the same category as the traditional Japanese legend of Rashomon, an enigmatic tale of murder and rape told by four participants who give four different versions of the story. After more than 130 years of being told and retold, this saga of murder, madness, and a great gold bonanza in the Rocky Mountains persists as one of Alberta's most popular and most enduring legends.

The first version of the story appeared as a supposedly factual account in a Montana newspaper, the *Helena Daily Herald*, on 6 August 1870. It reported that a blacksmith named Frank "Lemmon" and an unidentified partner were prospecting along a gulch in the mountains 120 miles north of Montana's Flathead Lake when they discovered a "fabulous" quantity of gold worth fifteen to twenty dollars per pan. Before they could capitalize on their find, however, they were attacked by hostile Natives. "My partner was killed by the Indians about eighteen miles from the diggings—shot by the Blackfeet," said Lemmon. He added that he barely escaped with his life and subsisted on "rosebuds and serviceberries" until he reached the safety of a mission in northwest Montana.

The Helena newspaper reported that Lemmon later took a party of prospectors back to the area where he believed he had found the gold. But he was unable to determine the exact location of the gulch. The angry prospectors accused Lemmon of misleading them and returned to Montana, tired, broke, and discouraged.

The next newspaper reference to the gold find appeared in the *Calgary Herald* on 6 October 1886, sixteen years after the original report. It said that a party of prospectors was again searching for what it called "Lemon Gulch," now said to be located somewhere along the Elk River on the British Columbia side of the Continental Divide.

The *Herald*, recalling the original story of the elusive gold mine, said that a prospector named "Lemon" and his partner, now identified as "Old George," had found a "good prospect" in a stream in the mountains. Unlike the original story, however, the *Herald* version said that Old George was not killed by the Blackfeet but "shot in some quarrel, the cause of which was unexplained." The newspaper added that Lemon had since moved on to a prospecting location in the Sweetgrass Hills area of Montana, and that his partner's body had been "found and buried a year or two ago."

After the *Herald* report appeared, the story of the mysterious Lemon and his ill-fated partner assumed many forms and variations. On 9 March 1938, a Pincher Creek historian named Freda Bundy reported in the *Family Herald and Weekly Star*, a newspaper supplement distributed across Canada, that several versions of the Lemon story had been gathered from prospectors who spent years searching the mountains for the lost gold. Bundy wrote that all the stories placed the location of the lost mine on the Alberta side of the Continental Divide. Some accounts said the area of the discovery was along the Highwood River in what is now Kananaskis Country. Others said the lost mine was somewhere in the Crowsnest Pass. But Bundy had her doubts about these Alberta locations. "Neither trail, nugget or gold dust was ever found on the eastern slope of the Divide, and it was not for lack of seekers and explorers," she said.

Perhaps the most well known and most widely circulated version of the story was one that first appeared in the *Alberta Folklore Quarterly* in March 1946. Recorded by Senator Dan Riley, a former mayor of High River, it placed the mine's location firmly on the Alberta side of the Rockies. Riley based his account on information he received forty years earlier from a High River trading post operator named Lafayette French, for whom Riley had worked before going into politics. French had come from Pennsylvania to what is now Alberta in the early 1880s. He brought with him a map that he said Lemon had drawn for him, and spent the next thirty years trying to find the place indicated on the map as "the richest source of gold ever found in the vicinity of the Rockies."

According to the Riley account, Lemon and his partner —identified by French as "Blackjack" and characterized as "the best prospector in the West"—had travelled north from Montana in the spring of 1870 and looked for gold along the North Saskatchewan River southwest of Edmonton. Failing to find anything of value, they headed back south along "an old Indian lodge-pole trail" and discovered "showings of gold" in a mountain stream flowing somewhere between High River and the Canada–United States border. They then followed the stream to its headwaters, dug two holes in the ground, and found a motherlode of gold-bearing rock "that was incredibly rich."

Riley said that the two men argued about whether or not they should winter at the site. Lemon settled the argument by killing his partner with a blow to the head from his axe. When he reached Montana, Lemon confessed his crime to a priest who dispatched a man named John McDougall to the scene to bury the body and mark the spot with a mound of stones.

Lemon spent the winter at the priest's mission and then agreed to accompany a party of prospectors back to the site. However, he was unable to find the location. According to Riley, local Natives had removed the mound of stones and obliterated all traces of the murder. The angry miners accused Lemon of deliberately misleading them. He became agitated to the point of turning "violently insane" and the party returned to Montana empty-handed.

The following year, 1872, the priest called on McDougall to lead another group of prospectors back to the place where he had buried Blackjack's body. They were supposed to rendezvous near the Crowsnest Pass and proceed north from there. However, McDougall started drinking whiskey on the night before he was due to leave, and drank himself to death.

The priest commissioned two more searches for the lost gold before abandoning the quest. One was aborted when the gold-seekers found their way blocked by a forest fire. The other involved Lemon himself, who became increasingly agitated when he approached the area where he had murdered his partner, and refused to continue with the search. Lemon retired to his brother's ranch in Texas where, according to Riley, he had "lucid intervals but never fully recovered his reason." During one of those lucid intervals he drew the map—a rough pen-and-ink sketch of rivers and mountain ranges—that

Lafayette French brought with him to Alberta in the 1880s. In the centre of the map was a cross marked with the word "Gold," at the head of a stream with three forks. The cross, said French, represented the location of the Lost Lemon Mine, and he vowed to search for it "as long as I have breath in my body."

Riley accompanied French on several prospecting trips during the years that he worked at French's High River trading post. He said that many of the trips ended tragically with one or more of the search party suddenly taking ill or dying. "Some strange hoodoo seemed to haunt all those who sought the lost mine." Indeed, bad luck followed all of French's attempts to find the mine over a thirty-year period.

However, when French took his last trip into the mountains shortly before his death in 1912, he claimed it was successful. He wrote a letter to a friend saying he had finally located the Lost Lemon Mine and was about to become very rich. However, before he could capitalize on his find—or disclose the whereabouts of the elusive bonanza—he was badly burned in a fire at his cabin near High River and died soon afterwards. "If he had actually solved the mystery which had occupied so many years of his life, the secret died with him," said Riley.

The search for the Lost Lemon Mine continued without success during the years after French's death. A few people returned from prospecting trips to say they were close to pinpointing the location, but nobody ever came back with any hard evidence of gold existing in the mountains. Several of these expeditions were bankrolled by Riley, who seems to have been drawn more to the romance of the quest than to the possibility that the mine might actually exist. "It's a good story," he said shortly before his death in 1948. "And why ruin a good story?"

While a few gold-seekers continued to venture hopefully into the mountains after Riley's death, the story gradually faded from public view until January 1989, when a geological technician from Edmonton named Ron Stewart announced that he had discovered gold in the Crowsnest Pass. The news made headlines around the world. Could this, finally, be the fabled Lost Lemon Mine? Stewart was quick to say he didn't think so. For one thing, there was only a microscopic quantity of gold in the volcanic rocks that he sampled. Stewart's discovery was a far cry from the bonanza that Lemon and his partner had supposedly stumbled upon in 1870. But Stewart did think there might be a connection between his find and that of the two old prospectors. He figured that Lemon and Blackjack could have found their fabled El Dorado somewhere along the thirty-mile strip of rocks that geologists call the "Crowsnest Volcanics."

Stewart's find leads to the following question: Why, during more than a century of searching, had no other prospectors come upon the rich find that Lemon apparently made? Because, reasoned Stewart, they were looking for what could not be seen with the naked eye. They were panning for gold in the traditional manner, sluicing crushed rocks and gravel for visible gold, whereas the gold they were seeking was virtually invisible, detectable only by modern geochemical scanning tools. Lemon and Blackjack's bonanza, if it existed, could have been an abnormal outcropping of visible gold on the surface of volcanic rocks that kept most of their treasure hidden within.

The Stewart discovery sparked a minor gold rush in the Crowsnest Pass, but it soon fizzled out when the latter-day fortune hunters discovered that the gold wasn't lying about on the ground or in streams waiting to be recovered. And while gold values of fractions of an ounce per ton might have been enough to excite Stewart and his colleagues at the University of Alberta's geology department, they were much too low to warrant commercial exploitation.

The Lost Lemon Mine remains a part of the lore of the Crowsnest Pass. Old-timers still tell the story to their grandchildren, drugstores sell books and pamphlets chronicling the tale, and one of the local campgrounds proudly bears the name, Lost Lemon R.V. Park. Whether the story is fact or legend will likely never be known. But as long as there remains a possibility that a treasure trove of gold exists somewhere in those hills, there will be adventurers willing to search for what Alberta historian Tom Primrose calls a "magic mine whose existence has never been fully accredited nor entirely disproved."

Father Lacombe: Apostle of the Natives—1883

(GLENBOW ARCHIVES NA-1654-1)

Father Albert Lacombe with Chief Crowfoot (left)
and Three Bulls: "Let the white people pass through
your lands and let them build their road."

FATHER ALBERT LACOMBE was a beloved nineteenth-century Roman Catholic missionary who spent more than thirty years bringing the faith, schools, and social services to what he called "the children of the plains." Of all the stories told about him, two have become the stuff of legend. The first is about his short-lived appointment as president of the Canadian Pacific Railway. The second is about his heart, which was preserved and venerated for more than seventy-five years after his death. Both stories are linked to the special relationship he had with the Natives of Western Canada.

Having a trace of Native blood in his veins became his passport to success as a missionary when Lacombe came west from Quebec as a 24-year-old oblate priest in 1852. The Ojibwa had kidnapped his great-grandmother when she was sixteen and while in captivity she had given birth to two mixed-race children, one who became Lacombe's maternal grandmother. He used his Native heritage to endear himself to the Fort Edmonton Metis when he first worked among them, and he later established a similarly good rapport with the Plains Cree, Assiniboine, and Blackfoot (now Siksika) tribes. He spoke their languages and earned their respect. The Blackfoot called him "the man of the good heart" (which seems both appropriate and ironic, given what happened to it after his death), and the Cree called him "the man of the beautiful soul."

In 1883, when the construction crews of the Canadian Pacific Railway reached what is now Alberta on their journey toward the Pacific Ocean, Father Lacombe was serving as pastor at the St. Mary's missionary post in Calgary that later became the cathedral seat of a sprawling Roman Catholic diocese that now extends from Drumheller to Lethbridge. Although by this time he did his pastoral work in the white community, he still maintained strong links with the local Blackfoot, Blood (now Kainai), Stoney, and Sarcee (now Tsuu T'ina) tribes.

The approaching railway alarmed the Blackfoot. They feared it would pass directly through their reserve, 110 kilometres southeast of Calgary. This they believed was a violation of Treaty Seven, the 1877 agreement that granted them protected reserve land and various concessions in return for opening up the bulk of their ancestral hunting grounds to settlement. The Natives warned the CPR construction crews that if they advanced into Blackfoot territory, more than seven hundred armed warriors would be ready to attack. The workers disregarded the warning. They also ignored Father Lacombe's plea that they stop work on the project until some kind of compromise could be reached. "It's no business of yours," said one worker.

Lacombe sent a telegram to federal Indian Commissioner Edgar Dewdney asking him to come as soon as possible because the situation was serious. In the meantime he took it upon himself to try and appease the angry Blackfoot. He met on the reserve with Chief Crowfoot, his friend for twenty years, and asked him to convene an emergency council of the warriors. The priest brought with him a large consignment of sugar, tobacco, tea, and flour, which he distributed to the Natives before addressing them.

"Let the white people pass through your lands, and let them build their road," said the black-robed missionary. "They are not here to rob you of your lands. They are only workers who are obeying their chiefs, and it is with these chiefs that you must settle your difficulties."

Lacombe assured the Natives that Commissioner Dewdney would meet with them in a few days to listen to their complaints and offer a solution. The priest took a big gamble when he did this. Dewdney had made no commitment to visit the reserve, and the priest was making a promise that the commissioner might or might not honour. Fortunately, however, the commissioner recognized that Lacombe had defused a potentially explosive situation, and he did meet with the Blackfoot a few days later. He offered them land on the south side of the Bow River in exchange for the land that the railway was taking from the reserve. Crowfoot urged the warriors to accept the offer and the railway construction proceeded without further incident.

The first train reached Calgary on 13 August 1883. The

following day Father Lacombe was surprised to receive a telegram from Winnipeg inviting him to have lunch in the private rail car of George Stephen, the president of the CPR Other dignitaries at the lunch included the presidents of three American railways, the CPR's general manager William Van Horne, and railway financier Donald Smith, who would later achieve immortality as the central figure in Canada's best-known photograph when he drove the last spike in the world's longest stretch of railroad. All wanted to thank Father Lacombe for averting a crisis on the Blackfoot reserve and for helping to keep the CPR construction on schedule. "I supped, or rather dined, with princes, lords and counts," wrote the priest afterwards in a letter to his archbishop. "The champagne flowed like the clear water of our river, and I obtained many favours of these gentlemen."

One of the favours given to Father Lacombe was a lifetime pass on the CPR for "Father Lacombe and an assistant." The priest rarely used the pass himself. He loaned it to friends who needed to travel by train. Among them were two members of the Sisters of Charity of Providence who often travelled together. A bemused train conductor would look at the pass, then at the sisters, and politely inquire, "And which one of you is Father Lacombe?"

Another of the favours was a whimsical decision by Stephen to resign his position as CPR president and appoint Father Lacombe in his place—for one hour. The priest returned the favour by appointing Stephen pastor of St. Mary's parish—also for one hour. Stephen accepted the honorary appointment with mock solemnity. Glancing out the car window at the new townsite, he murmured, "Poor souls of Calgary, I pity you."

Father Lacombe consolidated his reputation as a peacemaker during the 1885 Riel Rebellion when he used his influence to persuade Crowfoot and his fellow Blackfoot chiefs not to join the rebellion. A relieved and appreciative Sir John A. Macdonald invited Lacombe and the chiefs to a formal reception in Ottawa to thank them personally for their loyalty.

The missionary priest spent the last part of his life at the Lacombe Home for the Poor in what is now the south Calgary suburb of Midnapore, then a separate town. He opened the home in 1910 as a refuge for the orphaned and the elderly, and said he wanted it to be an institution devoted to the care of everyone, regardless of religion. It would be run by the Sisters of Charity of Providence, a nursing order of nuns (later renamed Sisters of Providence) whose successors still operate a seniors' nursing home on the site.

Shortly before Father Lacombe's death in 1916 at age eighty-nine, he said he wanted to leave his heart in Blackfoot country. Someone must have taken him literally at his word because Lacombe's heart was removed from his body before he was buried in St. Albert, where he had established a mission in 1861. According to some published accounts, the heart was then buried somewhere on the Blackfoot reserve east of Calgary but it was, in fact, preserved for the next seventy-six years by the Sisters of Providence. For fifty of those years they kept the heart on display in a shrine on the altar of a small chapel in the original Lacombe Home. Then, they moved the heart to the boardroom of what is now the Father Lacombe Care Centre, where they kept it in a cabinet under lock and key. Visitors who knew about it could make an appointment to view the sacred relic in its transparent chalice-like container, but most people were unaware of its existence because the sisters didn't promote it as a tourist attraction. The only Canadian sacred heart then known to be available for public viewing was that of Brother André Bessette at St. Joseph's Oratory Catholic Church in Montreal.

The Sisters of Providence kept Father Lacombe's heart until September 1992, when they finally decided to lay it to rest. "It was time to break with old Catholic tradition," explained Sister Margaret McGovern. At the time of Father Lacombe's death it had been common for Roman Catholics to venerate the body parts of saintly people. But times had changed and so had Catholic practices. The sisters held a private memorial ceremony at a small cemetery near the Home. Two Oblate priests carried a small coffin to the grave, said some quiet prayers, and buried Father Lacombe's heart forever. It lies beneath a small stone that says, "Here Rests his Heart."

(GLENBOW ARCHIVES NA-795-6)

A Jack the Ripper in Calgary—February 1889

John Innes sketch of Justice Charles B. Rouleau:
"You have come within a hair's breadth
of ending your life on the scaffold."

⚜

THE MOST SENSATIONAL murder case in the history of frontier Calgary almost ended in a miscarriage of justice. An all-white jury showed more sympathy for the sadistic white killer—who used his bare hands to mutilate his victim—than it did for the unfortunate Native female he killed. However, the judge refused to accept the jury's not-guilty verdict—which he knew was motivated by bigotry —and sent the case to a second jury for what he hoped would be a more principled decision.

Calgary had seen very little serious crime before this case hit the headlines in 1889. Only three murders had been reported in the immediate vicinity of the community during the six years after Calgary's establishment as a railway settlement in 1883, and two of them were fairly routine drunken-brawl crimes involving robbery and stabbing.

The man accused of murdering the Native woman was William "Jumbo" Fisk, a powerfully built thirty-two-year-old blacksmith from Iroquois Falls, Ontario, who was nicknamed after the big elephant in P. T. Barnum's famous circus. He moved west in 1882 and worked on a Canadian Pacific Railway construction crew. When the CPR reached Calgary in August 1883, Fisk put down roots in the area. He leased a ranch but soon lost it because, according to the *Calgary Tribune*, he "got into bad company and was given to gambling." Fisk then sold whiskey for a living and was arrested several times for public drunkenness.

In 1885, Fisk volunteered for service with the Alberta Field Force to fight in the Riel Rebellion. He lost a finger during a skirmish with the Frog Lake Cree. When he returned to Calgary he became part owner of the Turf Club, a rundown saloon very popular with poker players. It was located near the intersection of today's Centre Street and Stephen Avenue Walk. The frontier city then had a population of about twenty-four hundred.

In January 1889, Fisk sold his interest in the Turf Club to pay off his gambling debts. He moved to the Banff area to try his luck playing poker with the coal miners from nearby Anthracite, a mining shantytown that existed from 1886 to 1904. When he returned to Calgary, on 28 February 1889, he engaged the services of a young Native prostitute, Rosalie New Grass, and left her to die of injuries so horrific that the local newspapers opted not to describe them in detail.

New Grass was a member of an impoverished Cree community that lived on the western outskirts of Calgary. The men of the community eked out a meagre livelihood doing casual work for farmers and ranchers in the area. Some of the women, including New Grass, worked in town as prostitutes. A sense of the white community's antipathy toward them can be gleaned from the *Calgary Herald*'s description of Rosalie New Grass as a "very dissolute young squaw."

Fisk gave himself up within hours of the murder. He told the town's police chief, Matthew Dillabough, that he had taken New Grass to a room above the Turf Club "for immoral purposes" and that she had died "on my hands." But he would not admit that he killed or mutilated her. He said he left the room to have dinner and that when he returned, he found the woman lying on the bed covered in blood.

The *Herald*, the *Tribune*, and the *Lethbridge News* compared the Calgary case to the Jack the Ripper killings in England, which had been in the news over the previous six months. The Ripper, who was never identified, had murdered and eviscerated at least six prostitutes in the Whitechapel area of East London between August and November 1888. Those crimes, said the *Tribune*, seemed mild in comparison to the "fiendish brutality" demonstrated by the Calgary killer. "Jack, in most cases, cut his victims' throat first and did the mutilation with a knife afterwards. This brute, whoever he is, perpetrated his atrocities with his hand while his victim was still alive."

Fisk's story about finding the young woman covered in blood after he returned from dinner began to unravel when the Turf Club bartender, George Kelsey, gave evidence at a coroner's inquest. Kelsey said Fisk bought a round of drinks for the men at the bar before borrowing a dollar from Kelsey to take the young woman upstairs to Kelsey's bedroom. When he heard "a kind of groaning" coming from the bedroom at around 5:30 PM, Kelsey locked the bedroom door so that the couple would not be disturbed. Half an hour later he heard knocking on the ceiling, and he went upstairs to let Fisk out. He noticed that Fisk had blood on his face. When he entered the bedroom, Kelsey saw blood on the wall and on the bedclothes. "I think the squaw is dead," said Fisk. Kelsey put his ear to the woman's mouth and said, "I think I can hear her breathing."

They did not seek medical help for the woman. They left, and Kelsey suggested to Fisk that he wash the blood from his face before going downstairs. Fisk said he was hungry and headed out to dinner at the nearby Windsor Hotel. Kelsey joined him after first stopping at the bar for a drink. When they returned to the Turf Club a couple of hours later, Rosalie New Grass was dead. "I can't see what killed her unless it was heart disease," said Fisk. Kelsey told Fisk to turn himself in.

The coroner's jury found that "Rosalie, the young Cree squaw, came to her death from violence at the hands of William Fisk." The accused was remanded in custody until the trial started on 8 April 1889, before Judge Charles Rouleau of the Supreme Court of the North-West Territories. (Calgary was part of the territories until Alberta became a province in 1905.) Kelsey was also kept in custody; police considered him a possible accessory after the fact and feared he might skip town before the trial.

The trial was held in a large immigration shed adjoining the CPR tracks, about three blocks from the scene of the crime. Hundreds of Calgarians waited in line hoping to gain admittance. The *Lethbridge News* reported that the spectators included merchants, doctors, manufacturers, saloon keepers, teamsters, and "professional loafers with ears, eyes and mouths wide open." Most had to remain outside and settle for catching a glimpse of the proceedings through the windows.

Two lawyers defended Fisk. Calgary lawyer Ed Davis was joined by Frank Tyrell, a criminal lawyer from Morrisburg, Ontario, who appeared at the request of Fisk's widowed mother. They said that the evidence against Fisk was mostly circumstantial. They acknowledged that he had been with New Grass but argued that he did not cause her death. However, in one of the trial's most dramatic moments Fisk's guilt seemed to be confirmed. A North-West Mounted Police officer testified that one of the bloodstains on the bedroom wall was the imprint of a hand with one finger missing. The judge directed Fisk to hold up his left hand and the courtroom spectators gasped when they saw that the little finger was missing.

Despite this evidence, a succession of character witnesses, including former Calgary mayor George Murdoch, testified that Fisk was quiet, inoffensive, and kindhearted and "would not do injury to anyone." Defence lawyer Davis added that "only the most brutal man" could have murdered New Grass and that Fisk certainly did not fit this category. However, other witnesses recalled Fisk's "morbid interest" in the newspaper reports describing the Jack the Ripper murders.

In the end, Judge Rouleau had harsh words for both Fisk and Kelsey. In his charge to the jury he expressed disgust that Kelsey could "so violate the principles of morality as to allow a man to take a woman to a room in the house for such a purpose," and he criticized the "inhumanity and cruelty of both men" when they left the woman in the room without seeking medical assistance.

The jury deliberated throughout the Friday afternoon and sent out two messages during the evening that they could not agree on a verdict. The following morning they shocked everyone in the courtroom by finding the accused not guilty. Judge Rouleau refused to accept the verdict, saying it constituted a "denial of justice," and sent the jury back to chambers to reconsider. They returned an hour later and the foreman said they now could not agree on a verdict. The foreman also admitted that not every juror had agreed with the original not-guilty verdict. The judge dismissed them and ordered a new trial in the Supreme Court's July session.

The *Tribune* was disgusted with the jury's inability to reach a guilty verdict: "The evidence for the defence, without a syllable from the prosecution, would have been sufficient to convict the prisoner." The paper added that the initial not-guilty verdict seemed to be racially motivated. "The idea which seems to possess the minds of some people—that because a crime or offence is committed against an Indian, therefore the crime is lessened—is inhuman in the extreme."

At the second trial a new jury of nine men reviewed the same evidence. Judge Rouleau told them to forget the murdered woman's race and consider only the evidence at hand. "It made no difference whether Rosalie was white or black, an Indian or a Negro," said the judge. "In the eyes of the law every British subject is equal."

The jury took little more than two hours to reach a verdict: manslaughter. The jurors had taken into account the judge's statement that murder would only apply if they thought the accused had malicious intent. If there was no malicious intent, the judge said, the verdict should be manslaughter. "Thank goodness we were able to secure a sufficiently intelligent jury, who were able to tell the difference between black and white, which the former jury were utterly incapable of doing," commented the *Tribune*.

Judge Rouleau told Fisk he had "come within a hair's breadth of ending your life on the scaffold" and sentenced him to fourteen years of hard labour at Stony Mountain penitentiary in Manitoba. The judge said he did consider giving the accused a life sentence but changed his mind because members of Parliament and "other influential persons" made representations to the court about Fisk's "previous good character." The judge also took into account Fisk's service to his country and, above all, his "aged and sorrowing mother." Bob Edwards, editor of the *Eye Opener* newspaper, was not impressed by the judge's decision. He said that even a life sentence would not have been punishment enough. "Fisk got off with fourteen years but he should have been hanged."

Waterton Lakes Oil Boom— September 1902

John "Kootenai" Brown:
"There is quite an oil boom here. What am I to do?"

22

ALBERTA'S FIRST OIL boom occurred not in Turner Valley or Leduc—the sites of the province's best-known oil strikes—but in what is now Waterton Lakes National Park. The man who promoted the region's potential as an oil resource was a most unlikely petroleum pioneer—an Irish-born frontiersman in a fringed buckskin jacket and a wide-brimmed western hat, who simultaneously conducted a campaign to protect Waterton's wilderness and wildlife.

His name was John George Brown, nicknamed "Kootenai" Brown because he traded with the Kootenai tribe when panning for gold in what is now British Columbia during the 1860s. Born in Ennistymon, County Clare in 1839, this Irish adventurer came to Canada after serving with the British army in India, and in 1877 became one of the first white settlers in the Waterton Lakes area (then called Kootenai Lakes). He operated a trading post and supplemented his income by hunting, fishing, and guiding the occasional visitors to the region. In 1885, during the Riel Rebellion, Brown took time out to serve as head scout with the Rocky Mountain Rangers, a peace-keeping cavalry. He returned to Waterton in 1887, and established a homestead and ranching operation on the shores of what is now Lower Waterton Lake, close to the Canada–United States border.

In 1888, Brown started telling people about oil seepages he had discovered near today's Cameron Lake, adjoining Akamina Parkway. Local Natives had long known about these "stinking waters" but found no practical use for them. Brown became the first white man to exploit the seepages by soaking up the oil in gunny sacks to use as a lubricant for his wagons, as medicine for his horses, and perhaps as a fuel. One of the apocryphal tales about Brown (supposedly based on an affidavit he gave to a lawyer in Pincher Creek) says that he even mixed the oil with molasses, served it as a cocktail to the Stoneys, "and told them if they ever tasted or smelled anything like it, to be sure to let him know." (This piece of charming fiction actually made it onto the soundtrack of the 1966 Oscar-winning National Film Board feature, *Helicopter Canada.*)

In addition to using the oil himself, Brown sold it to his neighbours for a dollar a gallon. One of his casual employees, William Aldridge, devised a crude collection system similar to the sluice-box operations used in gold mining, which drew the oil into pits or strategically placed barrels. Using this method they were able to collect up to fifty gallons a day, which they sold to local ranchers for use in lamps and as lubricants.

As word of the oil discovery spread, speculators began staking claims in large numbers around the general vicinity of the seepages. The *Macleod Gazette* reported in August 1889 that "coal oil fever" was rampant. "There is a general feeling, which we think is justified, that this coal oil find is going to be a great big thing for the country." Two months later, the paper reported that a representative of Standard Oil had visited the area and had confidently predicted that oil would be found "in paying quantities."

While the *Gazette* promoted the oil discovery, and called for "capitalists" to develop the resource, the *Lethbridge News* urged caution. It praised the scenic splendour and wilderness charm of the area, and said it should not be spoiled by commercial development. "The government would do well to lay out a small national park, and so preserve the natural beauty of the surroundings."

Brown, too, could see that more speculators and developers flooding into the area would result in a negative impact on the wildlife and natural resources. Yet he had to accept some of the blame for the influx of newcomers because not only did he publicize the presence of oil near the Waterton Lakes, but he also spoke of the precious minerals that he found during his expeditions into the mountains. An exaggerated account of his prospecting activities appeared in the *Gazette* in September 1892, claiming that one of his quartz samples represented a discovery with "a potential worth of a million dollars."

Initial commercial attempts to exploit the Waterton oil discovery proved unsuccessful. Drill rigs tested to a depth of seventy metres and found only water. It wasn't until September 1902, when the

Rocky Mountain Development Company brought in a larger rig and drilled to a depth of 310 metres, that oil started flowing from Western Canada's first "discovery well." The area by that time had been designated as a federal forestry reserve, and Brown, at age sixty-one, was hired by the government as a part-time fisheries officer to patrol the lakes during the fishing season and report on water and weather conditions.

The oil strike occurred near Cameron Creek, just a few miles from Brown's cabin. While he did profit modestly from the strike when he sold a quarter section of his land to an oil company for two thousand dollars, Brown did not view this as a reason for changing his frontier lifestyle. He continued with his daily routine of hunting, fishing, and breaking horses for sale to the North-West Mounted Police.

The discovery well initially produced a steady flow of about three hundred barrels a day. That was enough to precipitate the beginnings of a shantytown development, optimistically dubbed Oil City. A townsite was cleared, streets were surveyed, and buildings were constructed, including a bunkhouse, dining hall, cabins, and even the foundations for a small hotel. Brown wrote in his diary on 24 October 1904 that he and his wife Isabella rode into the area "and saw lots of oil." He subsequently recorded that he bought thirteen gallons of crude from the drill site.

The flow from the first well dwindled to a trickle within a few years, leading to later suggestions by some industry analysts that it was, in fact, a "salted" well, perhaps fraudulently charged with extraneous oil to make the source appear more valuable than it actually was. Rocky Mountain Development drilled two more wells on the site but both came up dry. A new group, Western Oil and Coal Company, then took up the hunt. It drilled at the foot of Cameron Falls in the present Waterton townsite, also with disappointing results. The company did hit oil at a depth of 520 metres but the flow was a mere one barrel per day. That venture came to an end when the well walls caved in.

Despite the oil companies' failures, the lure of oil continued to attract hordes of speculators to the area. More than half of the forest park reserve had been reserved for petroleum exploration by 1905. This prompted local conservationists, including Brown, to appeal to the federal Department of the Interior to intervene. However, with new legislation for forest reserves pending, no remedial action was immediately taken to curb the oil hunters.

By 1908, Alberta's first oil boom had finally fizzled out and Oil City was abandoned. Brown added the title of provincial game guardian to his business card (which also described him as a "licensed guide, prepared to conduct tourists, hunters or prospectors in any part of the Rocky Mountains") and he became one of the prime movers in the process of transforming the forest reserve into a national park. In 1910, at age seventy-one, he was appointed forest ranger for the reserve. The following year he became acting superintendent of the newly established Waterton Lakes National Park, presiding over a protected wilderness and applying the rules of the Banff region (Canada's first national park) toward the development of visitor facilities.

Oil hunters continued to prospect in Waterton from 1911 onward. In 1914, Brown wrote to his superiors in Ottawa to say there was "quite an oil boom" in the district and that another company was about to start drilling within park boundaries. "What am I to do?" he asked. His superiors replied that he had the power under the recently adopted park legislation to reject any drilling applications he might receive.

Brown turned down the 1914 application but the pressure to commercially exploit the oil rights in the park did not end there. Over the next fifty years, a succession of would-be developers, spurred by the oil and gas discoveries in Turner Valley to the north, proposed schemes for Waterton that they hoped might be acceptable to the government of Canada. The most ingenious of these was a 1958 proposal to suck subterranean petroleum resources out of the park through a network of underground pipes introduced from outside the park boundary. As part of the proposed deal the federal government would be given royalties, thus making it a silent partner in the enterprise. Ottawa, however, was not buying. (Alberta, as the owner of the mineral rights, likely would have objected to this arrangement anyhow.)

Speculators continued to submit development proposals until 1963, when a published geologist's report finally dismissed the

26

notion that an oil bonanza might still exist in Waterton. The report concluded that the first discovery was probably oil from a distant underground reservoir that migrated along a fault plane and accumulated in sufficient quantity to appear to be the type of pool normally associated with a major strike. This report effectively ended all further attempts to revive the promise of Oil City, which had been destroyed by fire in 1919. However, there are those who still believe that if the sophisticated drilling technology of today had been available in 1902, Waterton Lakes might now be a vast oilfield instead of a national park. Producing wells located just north of the park have hit oil below 1,800 metres.

Brown served as acting superintendent of the park up to his death in 1916 at age seventy-six. One of his important tasks during that time was to facilitate the purchase by the Crown of the homestead property he had sold for two thousand dollars at the height of the oil boom. When the purchase was complete, the federal government owned all the property in the park and thus was able to control all future commercial enterprise and property development. Today the park is part of the Canada-United States Waterton-Glacier International Peace Park, jointly protected by the neighbouring countries and designated by UNESCO as a world heritage site. Canada also recognizes the Oil City location as a national historic site commemorating Western Canada's first producing oil well and the birthplace of today's oil industry.

The Mountain That Walked—April 1903

(GLENBOW ARCHIVES NA-3437-11)

Passengers emerge from the first train flagged
from danger after the slide at Frank:
"One of the most overwhelming disasters in
the history of the Dominion."

THE MOST DISASTROUS rockslide in Canadian history occurred at 4:10 AM on Wednesday 29 April 1903, when a massive chunk of Turtle Mountain collapsed into the Crowsnest Pass, swept through the frontier mining community of Frank, and killed at least seventy-six people. It could have been an even worse catastrophe if an intrepid brakeman for the Canadian Pacific Railway named Sid Choquette had not risked his life to warn an approaching passenger train of the imminent danger.

Choquette was working on a five-man rail crew, shunting coal cars on a spur line near the mine entrance on the eastern slope of Turtle Mountain, when suddenly the mountain started to move. He was lucky to escape. The locomotive engineer heard a deafening roar, looked up and saw an overhanging slab of rock break away, shatter into large boulders, and come crashing down the slope. The engineer gave the engine full throttle and yelled at his two brakemen—Choquette and Bill Lowes—to get aboard. They jumped onto the moving train as it lurched across the mine bridge. During the next ninety seconds, ninety million tons of rock fell behind them, smashing the bridge and tracks, sealing the mine entrance, and trapping twenty men inside.

When the trainmen arrived at the Frank station—a boxcar serving as a temporary facility until a permanent station could be built—they discovered that the Spokane Flyer, a westbound passenger train delayed by a snowstorm between Frank and Fort Macleod, was due to arrive at the slide scene within twenty minutes. The telegraph line was down so the station crew could not warn the Flyer that a wall of rock was blocking its path. But Choquette and Lowes had an alternative. They grabbed their lanterns and took off across the rubble to flag down the oncoming train.

Their lanterns barely pierced the darkness and the cloud of

overhanging rock dust as they clambered across the rocks, some of them still moving. Lowes had to give up in exhaustion after climbing for just a few minutes, but Choquette pressed on. He later estimated that some of the rocks were as big as three-storey apartment buildings. He had never encountered anything like it before. When he, too, was about to give up, after climbing for more than fifteen minutes, Choquette suddenly found himself tumbling down the eastern edge of the slide, right to the spot where the railway tracks emerged from the rubble. He landed there just in time. Lacerated, bruised, and exhausted, he waved his lantern and stopped the Spokane Flyer as it approached the slide. There were eighty passengers aboard the Flyer. They waited until daylight and then hauled their luggage around the rubble to resume their journey on a passenger train that came for them from the west.

The full scope of the catastrophe became apparent in the days following the slide. Initial press reports speculated that an earthquake or volcanic eruption had triggered an explosion in the mine. "One of the most overwhelming disasters in the history of the Dominion," reported the *Macleod Gazette*. Boulders travelling at an estimated sixty miles per hour had swept across the valley for a mile and climbed halfway up the slope on the opposite side. Houses, cottages, farms, a construction camp, and a livery stable were destroyed, and a section of the Oldman River was dammed.

At least seventy-six people, including seven women and twenty-one children, perished in the slide. Twenty-three were pulled alive from the rubble. The exact death toll would never be known. Only twelve bodies were ever recovered. Sixty-four individuals had listed addresses in Frank and were classified as missing and presumed dead. But the casualty toll was likely much higher because nobody ever calculated how many transient construction labourers and mine workers lived in tents and temporary shacks on the outskirts of the village near the mine entrance. One report said as many as fifty unidentified drifters could have been buried under the rubble.

Most of the inhabitants of Frank, totalling about seven hundred, were spared because much of the village lay outside the immediate path of destruction. But the force of the accompanying blast was so great that even those who were spared were thrown from their beds. The inhabitants fled to nearby Blairmore while shards of rock continued to shake loose from the mountain, and they stayed there for several days until the authorities told them it was safe to return home.

There were some miraculous escapes that day. One of the most dramatic was that of baby Marion Leitch, fifteen months old, who was sucked through a hole in the roof of her parents' home and thrown onto a bale of hay that had fortuitously landed nearby. Her two older sisters also escaped unharmed, but her parents and four brothers perished. Marion later moved to Nelson, British Columbia, married a man named Lawrence McPhail, and lived there until her death in 1977.

Another lucky escape awaited seventeen of twenty miners trapped below ground when the mine entrance was sealed. With their air supply dwindling, the men first tried digging with pickaxes and shovels through the wall of rock blocking the mine entrance, but abandoned that effort when they discovered that water from the Oldman River was seeping into the shaft. Then they tried crawling out an airshaft but found it blocked with boulders. Finally, they started digging a new shaft up through the soft coal. They worked in relays of two and three and, after thirteen hours, seventeen of them broke through to freedom. The other three died of respiratory failure while digging. One miner suffered a broken leg and had to be carried to safety on a makeshift stretcher. When he reached the village he made a terrible discovery: his house was destroyed and his wife and three children were dead.

The cause of the slide is still a subject of controversy. For more than seventy-five years the inherent geological instability of Turtle Mountain was seen as the main culprit. A 1904 federal Department of Interior report acknowledged that mining might have weakened the mountain but, that the most likely cause of the slide was the cumulative impact of rain and frost eroding what had long been known locally as an unstable body of sedimentary limestone rock. (Local Natives refused to camp at the base of Turtle Mountain, calling it "the mountain that walks.") This view of the Frank Slide as a natural disaster prevailed until 1979 when a member of the Crowsnest Pass Historical Society, James R. Kerr, released some private correspondence written in 1915 by the federal mines inspector, William Pearce. In a letter to a friend, the inspector alleged that efforts by the mine owners to promote their property in Europe as a low-cost coal producer, coupled with their reckless exploitation of the coal seam in the mountain, had set the stage for disaster.

Inspector Pearce noted that the Frank mine had been the first coal operation established on the Alberta side of the Crowsnest Pass, and that it ran for just two years before the slide occurred. The principal shareholders were H. L. Frank, a flamboyant mining promoter from Montana, and his partner Sam Gebo (sometimes known as Gibeau or Gibault), an American entrepreneur of French-Canadian origin. They launched their mining venture with a gala opening of the Frank townsite on 10 September 1901. On hand for the ceremony were North-West Territories premier Frederick Haultain and federal interior minister Clifford Sifton who, in the words of historian Frank W. Anderson, both made "proud speeches that everyone promptly forgot."

Inspector Pearce reported that the Frank colliery consisted of a series of huge underground chambers and near-vertical shafts sunk deep into the bowels of Turtle Mountain. The mine employed one hundred workers and at its peak capacity produced an average of two thousand tons of coal a day at a relatively cheap cost because the coal was easily accessible. "In some cases, it nearly mined itself," said one worker, noting that the coal was loosened by the earth tremors that occurred regularly in the mine, and that all the miners had to do was pick up the coal falling from the chamber ceilings.

By the beginning of 1903, promoters Frank and Gebo were pitching the property to potential buyers in France as an attractive investment opportunity and, according to inspector Pearce, were recklessly ignoring safety rules so they could pull as much coal out of the mine in the shortest time possible. "The result was there was not sufficient support left between the mine walls. Those walls coming together were what caused the slide." Pearce said he never had any doubt about what triggered the disaster, but that he couldn't go public with the information at the time because he "was there in an official capacity and could not express my views except confidentially." A public inquiry might have reached the same conclusion but none was ever held. This has led one historian, Allen Seager, to sur-mise that something like an official cover-up took place. Neither the federal nor territorial government wanted to take any action that might impede economic development or jeopardize investor confi-dence. What Seager calls a "seamless web of political patronage" in the administration of the Alberta coalfields effectively ensured that the politicians would not stand in the way of mine operators who wanted to maximize production and profits.

The community of Frank rebounded quickly from the disas-ter. People started to return to their homes nine days after the slide and the mine reopened about a month later, after what the mine own-ers called a "careful inspection" of Turtle Mountain. However, it soon became evident that the mine was far from safe. After monitoring the mountain for seven years—during which time there were two major fires in the mine and a new mine was opened north of the moun-tain—federal government inspectors warned in 1910 that the north slope of the mountain was in imminent danger of collapse and that mining should be discontinued. The company appealed to the provincial mines minister, Arthur Sifton, reminding him of the jobs and investments at stake. He responded by overruling the federal inspectors and declaring that mining could continue. (The threatened north-slope collapse never materialized.) But Sifton did decree that Frank residents should vacate the village for safety reasons. By 1914 the original townsite of Frank was deserted and a new village of the same name was established a few miles to the west.

The Frank mines generated large profits during the First World War because of high wartime demand for coal, but fires and other problems continued to plague the mining operation. In July 1918, the French owners shut down the mines for good. Promoter H. L. Frank had died in 1908—it was said—with a "mind broken by the memories of his ill-fated venture at Frank."

As for Sid Choquette, the heroic CPR brakeman who clam-bered over the rocks to warn the Spokane Flyer, he became the sub-ject of various false rumours, including one that the shock of the disaster caused him to lose his sanity, and another that he received a gold watch and a CPR guarantee of a job for life. The record shows, however, that the CPR just gave him a $25 cheque and a letter of commendation. He settled in Fort Macleod for a time, but eventually left the CPR to work for the Illinois Central Railroad. He remained with the ICR until his retirement in the 1930s.

The rocks of the Frank Slide still lie in the valley below Turtle Mountain, presenting a grim reminder of the 1903 disaster. It has been estimated that it would take one hundred gravel trucks, moving a total of three thousand tonnes per day, about sixty-six years to haul away the rubble. While the long-ago fear that the north slope might be the next to crumble and fall is no longer a concern, the "mountain that walks" is still considered to be potentially unstable. Alberta Environment officials warned in July 2002 that the south face of the mountain would eventually collapse—though they couldn't say when—and Crowsnest Pass residents started a fundraising campaign to install permanent seismic monitoring equipment on the mountain.

On 29 April 2003, while attending a memorial ceremony marking the one hundredth anniversary of the slide, Premier Ralph Klein both surprised and delighted the residents by announcing that his government would immediately spend $1 million on a monitoring system for the mountain. "It is just a matter of putting in leading-edge, state-of-the-art sensors to make sure there is lots of warning before the next slide," said Klein.

Alberta's Aviation
Pioneers—August 1907

(GLENBOW ARCHIVES NA-463-30)

Framework of experimental aircraft built by
brothers John, George, and Elmer Underwood:
"Another thousand dollars might have put the Underwood
brothers in the front ranks of the world's aerial pioneers."

THE FIRST AVIATORS to fly in a heavier-than-air plane in Canada were three farm boys from the Stettler district who built their machine out of barnyard scrap. But because they were unable to afford a forty-horsepower motorcycle engine to accomplish an officially recognized free flight, their names were never enshrined in Canadian aviation history. Instead, the credit for the first Canadian manned flight goes to an aviator named John McCurdy, who achieved his success with the financial backing of the famed inventor, Alexander Graham Bell.

The Alberta aviators were brothers John, Elmer, and George, the sons of North Dakota inventor John K. Underwood Sr., who patented the revolving disc harrow in 1872. He settled in the Stettler area, at a place called Krugerville Corners (which no longer exists), before the turn of the twentieth century. Underwood's sons joined him after trying their luck prospecting in the Yukon during the Klondike gold rush.

The boys inherited their father's flair for invention. Excited by the news that flights were being made in the United States by the self-taught inventors, Orville and Wilbur Wright, the Underwoods decided they would build their own plane. They hoped to win a contest for the first flight in the British Empire.

In the absence of available literature, they had to rely on their imaginations. The Wright brothers had refused to publish a description of their aircraft pending patent approval. At the time, little had been published on the subject of flight, apart from a treatise by a Nova Scotia-born mathematician named Simon Newcomb, who theorized (before the Wrights came along to prove him wrong) that while it might be possible for a large plane to carry a man in flight, a small light aircraft would never be strong enough. Newcomb's conclusion might have been enough to deter many would-be aircraft inventors, but not the Underwoods. They began looking for ways to build a machine that would be light, strong, and airworthy.

They began their experiments in May 1907 with kites and propellers driven by strong rubber bands. Not one of the brothers could have invented the airplane by himself, but collectively they achieved some creditable flights. John Underwood, a self-taught mathematician, created the designs. Elmer built the models and then a full-sized machine of laminated wood, canvas, old motorcycle wheels, and bicycle wheels. George, who was more enthusiast than inventor or builder, provided moral support and the physical push to get the 205-kilogram machine into the air.

By the beginning of July 1907, the Underwoods were ready to put their contraption on public display and they did so at the Stettler Exhibition. Looking for all the world like a forty-foot trampoline mounted over an open two-wheeled carriage, it attracted a fair amount of press attention, much of it inaccurate. The *Toronto Globe* characterized it as a "balloon" with a "gas bag 300 feet long." A Winnipeg newspaper, the *Manitoba Free Press,* reported that the machine was "equipped with 500 horse-power" like a flying locomotive or steamship. Only the local Stettler paper managed to give an accurate description of what was essentially a large fixed wing craft without fuselage or engine.

The Underwood machine never made it into the air during the Stettler Exhibition, but that didn't stop local businessmen from dreaming up promotional schemes. They told reporters that special trains might have to be chartered to bring people from across the prairies to witness the trial flights.

To test their invention the Underwoods built Canada's first airstrip in a field near their home. Because they had no engine they had to test it as a kite tethered to the ground with a 213-metre rope. The first test took place on 10 August 1907, with an audience of skeptical farmers on hand to witness the event. The results were encouraging. The brothers put five sacks of wheat weighing a total of 160 kilograms into the "cockpit" and achieved an impressive height of thirty metres with the wind blowing at thirty kilometres an hour. John then asked to be allowed to fly in place of the wheat sacks. At first, his brothers, fearing for his safety, refused. They relented when he suggested that they shorten the rope.

For fifteen glorious minutes John floated about three metres above the ground. He demonstrated the aircraft's ability to turn in the breeze and then drifted gently back to earth. Although it doesn't appear anywhere in the record books, this was undoubtedly the first time in Canada that a man flew in a kite. Aviation historian Frank Ellis acknowledged the achievement in his 1954 book, *Canada's Flying Heritage.*

Unfortunately, because the machine had no engine, it failed to qualify for the Empire Prize. The brothers began to experiment with a seven-horsepower motorcycle engine but soon realized they needed more power. They could taxi on their makeshift runway but they couldn't get the plane off the ground. They wrote away for an estimate on a forty-horsepower engine built by the Curtiss Motor Cycle Shop in Hammondsport, New York, and were shattered by the response: US$1,300.

The local member of Parliament took their case to Ottawa, asking that import duties be waived. But free trade wasn't on the government's agenda in those days. The Underwoods were out of luck. No engine, no prize, no glory. Eighteen months later, on 23 February 1909, John McCurdy won the race to become the British Empire's first aviator, flying a plane equipped with an engine from the Curtiss shop in Hammondsport. The historic flight took place over the frozen waters of Bras d'Or Lake at Baddeck Bay, Nova Scotia, near the summer home of Alexander Graham Bell who financed the experiment.

The Underwoods continued to fly their craft as a kite through the spring and summer of 1908, often on windy nights when the eerie light from the lantern they hung on the bobbing aircraft frightened travellers in the district. As time went on, they became more and more careless in their handling of the aircraft, eventually crashing it and damaging it beyond repair. Abandoning their dreams of further flight, the brothers piled the wreckage behind the barn and turned their minds to other things.

Elmer remained in the Stettler area and died during the 1940s. His brothers drifted southward to Kansas and eventually ended up in California. Only John continued to experiment as an inventor. In the late 1970s, when he was in his nineties, he was dabbling in the ancient art of alchemy, trying to convince the Smithsonian Institution that he could transmute lead into gold using an alfalfa extract as a catalyst.

To the end John maintained that the Underwood plane was capable of free flight. Aviation historian Ellis, who built a working replica of the machine during the 1930s, agreed. "The flying models made by the Underwoods proved beyond all doubt that their design was airworthy. It is frustrating to reflect that another thousand dollars might have put the Underwood brothers in the front ranks of the world's aerial pioneers."

"All Hell for a Basement" —October 1907

Canadian Pacific Railway depot at Medicine Hat with the town's black bear mascot, "Nancy," foraging in a pen near the station platform: "Don't ever think of changing the name of your town. It's all your own and the only Hat of its kind on Earth."

꧁꧂

THE NEWCOMERS WANTED to change the name of Medicine Hat to something plain and ordinary like Leopoldville or Smithville. The city had been the butt of some cruel weather jokes in the American newspapers, they said, and the Medicine Hat name looked positively ludicrous on the front of a chamber of commerce brochure. The *Calgary Herald* actively supported the idea of a name change, said the newcomers, so why not put the question to the ratepayers for a vote?

The old-timers were appalled. The name of their city was distinctive and steeped in romance and Native history, they said. It would be absurd to think of changing it. "I wish Rudyard Kipling knew of this," said one old-timer, Francis Fatt. "He would flay the hide off these blighters."

Kipling had a long-standing relationship with Medicine Hat, dating back to before its incorporation as a municipality, and the place rated something more than footnote status in the travel journal of the globetrotting author. In fact, though he didn't actually mention the place by name, Kipling did devote the better part of a chapter to Medicine Hat in his 1908 book, *Letters to the Family: Notes on a Recent Trip to Canada.* He observed that the city had been "born lucky" because it sat on top of a plentiful supply of natural gas that the city fathers had wisely co-opted for the use of the citizens. "Imagine a city's heating and light—to say nothing of power—laid on at no greater expense than that of piping," wrote Kipling.

He wrote the book after a 1907 lecture tour of Canada during which he was given a welcome comparable to that usually reserved for visiting royalty. Kipling was then at the height of his literary powers, with such acclaimed publications as *Kim* and *The Jungle Book* to his credit, and he was about to become the first British writer to receive the Nobel Prize for literature. In Canada, he took full advantage of his celebrity status to promote his view that this country should lead the way toward a new imperial order because the forces opposing the British Empire were making dangerous headway.

Before 1907, Kipling had paid two visits to Medicine Hat. On the first trip, in 1889, he seems to have been playing the role of a railway hobo. He was then twenty-three and on his way to London after working as a journalist in India for seven years. His rambling itinerary took him from China and Japan to San Francisco, and then up to Canada, where he stayed for a week before returning to the United States to take a train across the continent. Medicine Hat, he said, "was reached by me in a freight car, ticket unpaid for." He recalled a conversation that he had upon arrival with a "broken-down prospector in a boxcar" who predicted that Kipling would hear more about the town that was "born lucky." Medicine Hat then had a population of about 250 and it served as a maintenance and repair stop for the locomotives of the Canadian Pacific Railway.

Medicine Hat was still two years away from incorporation when Kipling paid his second visit to the railway hamlet, in 1892. This time he was travelling with his American wife, the former Caroline Balestier, on a honeymoon trip around the world. When they arrived in Canada, after taking the train north from St. Paul, Minnesota, to Winnipeg, they found the country "deep in snow." Kipling didn't particularly enjoy the train ride across the Prairies. "The tedium of it was eternal," he said. But he was charmed by this hamlet with the strange name that he had visited three years earlier. "The only commonplace thing about the spot was its name —Medicine Hat—which struck me instantly as the only possible name such a town could carry." He also noted that the townsfolk kept a live black bear named Nancy in a pen near the train station, and that the community boasted a "painfully formal public garden."

Kipling almost didn't make it to Medicine Hat when he revisited Canada in 1907. His lecture tour itinerary did not include a scheduled appearance in what was, by that time, a vibrant city of six thousand. However, when the Medicine Hat city fathers heard that Kipling was in the country and might not be visiting their city, they sent him a telegram asking him to change his travel plans and stop there on his way home. Kipling agreed and he arrived in Medicine

Hat on 13 October. He did not give a lecture there but he did give an interview to the *Medicine Hat News* in which he said—referring to the city's treasure trove of natural gas—"This part of the country seems to have all hell for a basement and the only trapdoor appears to be in Medicine Hat." The phrase became one of Kipling's literary legacies to the young city. When Medicine Hat published its centennial history in 1983, one hundred years after the railway arrived, it titled the book *All Hell for a Basement.*

Also in the interview with the *Medicine Hat News*, Kipling commented on the community's unconventional name. "Don't ever think of changing the name of your town," he said. "It's all your own and the only Hat of its kind on Earth."

Three years later, in November 1910, however, a group of citizens began discussions on changing the name. They were a dissident minority on city council, representing the city's real estate and industrial interests. They thought a name change was in order because Medicine Hat had become synonymous with bad weather in the minds of certain American newspaper commentators. North America's most northerly weather station happened to be located in Medicine Hat, making it easy for American newspapers to blame the city for all the blizzards that came down from the north in the winter.

That was one knock against the name, said the council dissidents. Another was the fact that the name seemed to be a turnoff for potential business investors. "After all," said one alderman, "how could one take a place named Medicine Hat seriously?"

When the dissidents decided to make the proposed name change the subject of a city plebiscite, the old-timers in the community became alarmed. Postmaster Francis Fatt undertook to write to Kipling to tell him what was happening. "We look to you as the Father Confessor of the Empire, and ask you to help us poor stragglers with advice." Fatt noted that the city's name, translated from the Cree, had "grown warm in our hearts" because of its long-time association with local courtships, marriages, the births of children, and the building of homes. Yet a group of newcomers wanted to change the name because of the "whacking lies (may God forgive them) of the U.S.A. newspaper men in regard to our weather and so forth . . . .

Can you help us with a few words of encouragement in combatting these heretics?" asked Fatt. "Your influence here is great. If it is shown that you are against this proposition, it will help us materially."

Kipling was more than happy to provide a few words of encouragement. "I see no reason on earth why white men should be bluffed out of their city's birthright by an imported joke," he wrote. "Accept the charge [of causing bad weather] joyously and proudly, and go forward as Medicine Hat—the only city officially recognized as capable of freezing out the United States and giving the continent cold feet."

As for the unusual nature of the Medicine Hat name, Kipling noted that several American towns and cities—Schenectady, Podunk, Schoharie, Poughkeepsie—had names that were just as curious. Yet the citizens in these communities did not change the names, he said, because they respected the choices made by their ancestors.

"To my mind, the name of Medicine Hat has an advantage over all the names I have quoted," wrote Kipling. "It echoes the old Cree and Blackfoot tradition of mystery and romance that once filled the Prairies. Also it hints, I venture to think, at the magic that underlies the city in the shape of your natural gas. Believe me, the very name is an asset, and as years go on will become more and more of an asset. It has no duplicate in the world; it makes men ask questions; it draws the feet of the young men toward it; it has the qualities of uniqueness, individuality, assertion and power. Above all, it is the lawful, original, sweat-and-dust-won name of the city, and to change it would be to risk the luck of the city, to disgust and dishearten old-timers, and to advertise abroad the city's lack of faith in itself. Men do not think much of a family that has risen in the world, changing its name for social reasons. They think still less of a man who, because he is successful, repudiates the wife who stood by him in his early struggles. I do not know what I should say, but I have the clearest notion of what I should think of a town that went back on itself."

Kipling concluded his letter by saying that the two arguments put forward for the name change were weak and unconvincing. "In the first case the town would change its name for fear of being laughed at. In the second, it sells its name in the hope of making more money under an alias or—as the *Calgary Herald* writes—for the sake of a name that 'has a sound like the name of a man's best girl and looks like business at the head of a financial report.'

"But a man's city is a trifle more than a man's best girl. She is the living background of his life and love and toil and hope and sorrow and joy. Her success is his success; her shame is his shame; her honour is his honour; and her good name is his good name.

"What, then should a city be rechristened that has sold its name? Judasville."

The letter, which was printed in full in the *Medicine Hat News*, had the desired effect. The name-change plebiscite was defeated by a margin of more than ten to one. The question was never raised again. Today, the local chamber of commerce likes to promote Medicine Hat as "the Gas City," while the rest of Alberta popularly refers to it simply as "the Hat."

Take a Bow, Sarah
Bernhardt—January 1913

THE ALBERTA NEWSPAPERS could hardly contain their excitement when the New York vaudeville impresario Martin Beck announced that the famed French actress Sarah Bernhardt would perform in Edmonton and Calgary while on a 1913 swing through Western Canada. "A year ago, the possibility of the Divine Sarah actually playing in Edmonton would have been cause for laughter," declared the *Edmonton Bulletin*. "But in these days of managerial enterprise, when nothing is too good for the vaudeville stage, one begins to expect almost everything." The *Calgary Herald* hailed Bernhardt as "the greatest acquisition to the American stage which its history has ever known" and looked forward to seeing a "stupendous programme of vaudeville" when she arrived in Calgary.

Bernhardt's visit to Alberta occurred during one of the many tours of North America that she undertook for financial reasons after her career in Europe began to falter. A dozen years earlier the acerbic George Bernard Shaw had written in the *Saturday Review* that he would "certainly not treat her as a dramatic artist of the first rank, unless she pays me well for it." But Alberta welcomed Bernhardt with open arms. "A red-letter day in the theatrical history of Edmonton," said the *Bulletin*. The *Edmonton Journal* noted that for those unable to see Bernhardt performing live at the Empire Theatre in Alexandre Dumas' *Camille* there would be an opportunity to see her on screen at the Empress Theatre in a silent-film version of Sardou's *La Tosca*.

The manager of the Empress had invited Bernhardt to "see herself act," and hoped that the famous star would attend.

Bernhardt was sixty-eight when she came to Alberta. She had injured her right knee while jumping off a parapet during a perform-ance in Rio de Janeiro eight years earlier, and by 1913 she was unable to walk unsupported. But her invincible spirit, and the need to keep making money to resolve her perpetual financial troubles, sustained her through several long and exhausting tours.

While she no longer had the energy to do a full-length, five-act play, she still had enough stamina to get through the final hour of *Camille* (a deathbed scene) at both the matinee and evening per-formances during her one-day stop in Edmonton. The local critics were impressed. "Though speaking in French, which was foreign to a majority of those present, the audience and Madame Bernhardt understood one another from the first liquid word that passed her scarlet lips until the curtain finally fell," said the *Bulletin*. The *Journal* observed that her film at the Empress had also been a success. Her tour manager provided a translation of Bernhardt's response: "My time in your city has been all too short, and I cannot help but open my heart to your people for the magnificent reception they have given me." The manager added that she had been too tired to take in the film during her visit, and would not be granting any press interviews. "Long journeys fatigue her."

The *Calgary Herald* began its front-page coverage of the Bernhardt visit a week before her arrival. "There are five kinds of actresses," said the newspaper, quoting Mark Twain. "Bad actresses, fair actresses, good actresses, great actresses, and Sarah Bernhardt." The rival *Albertan* noted sourly (and inaccurately) that Bernhardt was not really French, but a French-speaking native of Holland. (She was, in fact, of mixed French-Dutch parentage, born Rosine Bernard in Paris on 23 October 1844.) But the *Albertan* soon changed the tone of its reporting to reflect that of the *Herald*. "As befits the exalted position she occupies in the theatre world, she comes regally, in her own special train," the *Albertan* reported on the morning of 14 January 1913, as the Bernhardt company of twenty-five per-formers arrived from Edmonton. A *Herald* reporter returned from the train station and wrote that "Madame" was "in excellent fettle and growing literally younger every day."

Bernhardt gave four performances in Calgary, at the 1,504-seat Sherman Grand Theatre. All were sold out, with ticket prices ranging from twenty-five cents for a seat in the balcony to three dollars for a box seat. On 14 January, she gave matinee and evening performances of a scene from Victor's Hugo's *Lucrezia Borgia*. The following day, she performed the deathbed scene from *Camille*. Once again, the reviews were suffused with hyperbolic praise. "The personality of the great actress, her wonderful voice, and her lightning changes of expression united to make a stage presence which kept her audience enthralled," said the *Herald*. "An exposition of her marvelous histrionic powers which surpassed the fondest imagination of her most ardent admirer," said the *Albertan*.

Bernhardt also impressed the Calgary reporters when she met with them in her dressing room after the performance. "The obscure news writers were made to feel that Madame Bernhardt considered the honour was hers, so pronounced was the warmth and cordiality of her greeting," said the *Albertan*. Speaking through an interpreter, Bernhardt told the reporters she could hardly believe that an audience would give rise to "such pitches of enthusiasm" over a play presented in a language that few of them understood. "It is a surprise to me," she said. "And it is an exhibition of the culture of the Canadian public."

The actress endeared herself to the owners of a Calgary bakeshop, Confisserie Parisienne, when she declared that it reminded her of similar bakeries in Paris. "You should have seen the *gateaux* that I bought there. I almost thought I was home." But she didn't endear herself to local suffragists who, inspired by the example of Nellie McClung in Manitoba, had spent four years fighting for the same political rights as men. "A mistake," commented Bernhardt. "And more than that it is a physiological impossibility. Men are the natural leaders and lawmakers, and it is the height of folly for women to attempt to aspire to such positions." A *Herald* editorial nodded approval. "Madame Bernhardt has a knowledge and experience of the world which is wide as the horizon in comparison to the vision of a militant suffragette."

Bernhardt never returned to Edmonton but she did make it

back to Calgary for two days of performances at the Orpheum Theatre in June 1918. By that time her leg had been amputated and she was no longer front-page news, even in Calgary. The news was dominated by stories about German U-boats being sunk in the Atlantic, and American fighter planes flying over France. But the *Herald* did report that Bernhardt had done her bit for the war effort by making "numerous trips from Paris to the front since the Kaiser began his war against the world" and that she had been named a Chevalier (knight) of the French Legion of Honour.

For her second Calgary appearance Bernhardt chose, along with her ever-popular *Camille*, a one-act play with a wartime theme entitled *Du Théâtre au champ d'honneur* (From the Theatre to the Field of Honour). "The play is nothing more than a setting for the great actress," said the *Herald*. "The audience could not help but understand and appreciate the wonderful force and the unquenchable spirit that inhabit the frail body of the actress, who herself has suffered so much."

Bernhardt continued to act and tour for another five years after her second Calgary appearance, playing parts that she could perform while seated or lying down. She collapsed during a dress rehearsal of Sacha Guitry's *Un Sujet de roman* (A Subject of Romance) when she was in her late seventies, but recovered sufficiently to take on the challenge of a Hollywood film. "I will die on stage," she said. "It is my battlefield."

She died on 26 March 1923 at age seventy-eight, more or less as she had predicted, while making a film of Guitry's *La Voyante* (The Fortuneteller) at her Paris home. The *Calgary Herald*, recalling her visits to Alberta in 1913 and 1918, reported that she ended her life in poverty. "The tragedy of Bernhardt's passing is emphasized by these accoutrements of the 'movies' for which she was forced, at seventy-eight, to act because she was penniless."

Coal Mining Undermines Edmonton—1915-31

Riverdale home severely damaged by natural gas explosion: "Sills torn away from the windows to the extent that you could drop a cat in."

⚮

THE EDMONTON COMMUNITY of Riverdale looked as if an earthquake had hit it. Years of unregulated coal mining under the community had caused houses to slouch and crumble into their foundations, gas mains to fracture, sidewalks to buckle, and gaping fissures to appear in road surfaces. By 1930 such words as "collapse" and "depression," then being used to characterize the declining world economy, took on more sinister meanings when applied to Riverdale. Why did the community authorities allow this to happen? Because they had no legal remedies to prevent it. The below-ground mineral rights were "alienated from the Crown," which meant they belonged to private individuals or companies, and were not subject to the regulations laid down for lands whose mineral rights were retained by the federal or provincial governments. Because of this unregulated mining, a shady legacy still exists in the daily life of Riverdale residents.

From the end of the nineteenth century it had become apparent that coal mining might be beneficial for the economic development of the Edmonton region. In 1895, the *Edmonton District Directory* reported that coal "fully equal in quality" to the "black diamonds" found in Colorado and Wyoming was "first in value and importance among the economic minerals of Alberta." In 1910, a federal geologist predicted that Edmonton would become the centre of a flourishing mining industry because the coal seams dotting the steep banks of the North Saskatchewan River were capable of being "worked economically and on a commercial scale."

Riverdale, a residential district picturesquely nestled on the flats in a bend of the North Saskatchewan River, became the centre of the coal mining activity. The diggings formed a labyrinth thirty metres below the community. However, nobody raised the alarm because many Riverdale families depended on the mines for their livelihoods. The *Edmonton Bulletin* reported enthusiastically in March 1921 that there were few municipalities in the Dominion "where a real mine in full operation can be visited within a half mile of the city post office."

By 1924, some residents were beginning to have doubts about the wisdom of having coal mining directly under their homes. At the time, nobody could point to any evidence of major surface damage resulting from the mining, but there was a nagging suspicion that shifting foundations and cracks in basement walls might have been caused by something other than changes in the weather. After receiving several complaints of structural damage to homes, Edmonton city council commissioned an engineer, James Church, to study the impact of mining on the Riverdale community. But the elected officials had to tread cautiously because the coal industry was important to the local economy and they did not want to take any action that might result in jobs being lost. A city commissioner stressed the need to protect "any enterprise which materially contributes to the development of the city from an industrial standpoint."

Nevertheless, Church's report warned of "dire consequences" if the city didn't take action to halt the mining. The mayor and aldermen debated the issue at length and finally agreed to put community safety ahead of economic gain. But the city's hands were tied because the mineral rights to the land belonged to the mining company, Penn Coal, and were not subject to government regulation. All the city could do was urge the provincial government to pass legislation prohibiting mining under city streets, and request compensation from the government for those residents whose homes were damaged by the mining.

The city itself became a mining casualty in 1926 when the Riverdale sewage disposal plant developed cracks in its treatment tanks and raw sewage spilled into the river. The Edmonton public school board became alarmed about the potential danger posed to Riverdale's Alex Taylor School, and asked the city to ensure that Penn Coal did nothing to jeopardize the school's safety. Penn Coal responded with an assurance that no mining would take place directly under school grounds.

Faced with a growing list of complaints from Riverdale

residents and its own mounting bills for repairs to the sewage plant and other damaged municipal property, the city finally began in 1926 to push for provincial legislation to stop mining under the community. The province took three years to respond, and then only to say "definite steps would probably be taken by the government toward instituting an inquiry into the alleged mining damage." In the meantime, Penn Coal continued to remove its "black diamonds" from under Riverdale as more and more accounts of serious structural damage to homes were received at city hall.

On 22 January 1930, the *Edmonton Journal* reported that a Riverdale family named McKay had awakened that day at 3 AM to the "unique and terrifying experience" of feeling their house sink beneath them. When the mayor and city commissioners visited the property, they found sagging floors, cracked walls, and sills "torn away from the windows to the extent you could drop a cat in." A few days later, the mayor and the city engineer visited another badly damaged Riverdale home, which the engineer promptly condemned as "unsafe for occupation."

In February 1930, the threat to Riverdale homes took on a horrific new dimension when two brothers, Vernon and Calvin Archer, were thrown across their basement while trying to light the furnace. Calvin, age twenty-one, was hospitalized after suffering burns to his hands and face. Vernon, age eighteen, also suffered bruises and burns but did not have to be hospitalized. City engineers subsequently determined that a gas main had broken near the house and that escaping gas had collected in the basement. The engineers also concluded that Penn Coal's mines caused the subterranean ground shifts that broke the gas main.

The *Edmonton Bulletin* reported in March 1930 that, as a result of the mining, Riverdale was full of "twisted fences, broken and cracked foundations, damaged roads and sidewalks, and huge cracks in the earth." Penn Coal responded by placing a full-page advertisement in the *Edmonton Journal* proclaiming its importance as an employer in the community. However, a month later it was forced to close one of its two Riverdale mines when the city declared that the buildings immediately above it were "or may become at any moment unsafe for human habitation."

Penn Coal continued to operate its second Riverdale mine while the province dragged its feet on introducing legislation to prohibit mining under cities and towns. Finally, in 1931, the province passed a bill to amend the Urban Mining Regulations Act, and Penn Coal was ordered to cease operations in Edmonton. But the government did not address the question of compensation to Riverdale residents for damage caused by the mines. It wasn't until February 1933, nine years after James Church first warned of the dangers of continued mining under Riverdale, that the province agreed to give the city $12,000 "in a compassionate allowance" with the understanding "that the government does not admit any liability whatsoever" with respect to the damage caused.

Although the city balked at accepting the $12,000, because it would pay for less than forty percent of the estimated structural damage to 115 homes, it was urged by Riverdale residents to ratify the settlement on their behalf. The president of the property owners association, Sidney Truscott, said that distributing the money "at this time of great depression would do a great deal more good to us now than it would for some future council to give it to our great-grandchildren in the far distant future." He had not worked since the closure of the Penn Coal mine, two years previously, and he said there were "hundreds of others who are in just the same position." When these beleaguered property owners appealed to the city for tax relief, they were told that any repairs to damaged homes would be viewed as improvements and so their property tax assessments would be going up, not down.

It took the city another six months to decide how to distribute the $12,000, which Truscott characterized as little more than a "band-aid on a massive wound." Although he had pressed for an early settlement "to render first aid in an admitted catastrophe," he said "you can scarcely blame the sufferer if he moans in the meantime."

The compensation package did help the community to rebuild, but the story of mining damage in Riverdale did not end there. In May 1935, the *Edmonton Journal* reported in a front-page story that members of the John Paike family narrowly escaped injury when their front yard collapsed into an abandoned mine below.

"It may happen again," warned the *Journal.* And even as recently as 1992, authors Allan Shute and Margaret Fortier were reporting in their book, *Riverdale: From Fraser Flats to Edmonton Oasis,* that the ground in Riverdale (where both authors live) was still giving way occasionally. "A faint reminder of what former Riverdalians had to endure."

Chautauqua in Western Canada—July 1917

John M. Erickson, the American promoter who introduced Chautauqua to Canada: "If Regina can be booked, then any town or city in Canada can be booked."

THE FIRST SCOUTING report was bleak. In the fall of 1916, an advance man for Chautauqua, the travelling tent show presentations of talk, drama, and music that had swept small-town America for more than fifteen years, came north to investigate the possibility of expanding the touring circuit into Western Canada. Named after the lake in New York state where the movement began in 1870, Chautauqua featured talented troupes of imported European opera singers, magicians, and actors. The shows were hugely popular in culturally isolated parts of the United States, satisfying the need for self-improvement and enter-tainment, but they had never been seen in Canada. And, at first, it didn't seem like they ever would be. After visiting towns in Saskatchewan and Manitoba, the Chautauqua scout wrote to his New York bosses saying, "There is not the remotest chance of doing any business here." Canada was at war and the mood in the country was grim. The country was too preoccupied with the conflict in Europe to give any attention to an untested form of entertainment.

That might have been the end of the story for Chautauqua in Canada were it not for the fact that another American Chautauqua promoter, thirty-four-year-old John Erickson, just happened to be visiting Alberta at about the same time, in October 1916. Erickson found a more receptive attitude toward Chautauqua in Lethbridge, where a lawyer named Samuel Dunham expressed interest in the edu-cational and entertainment aspects of the travelling cultural program. Would Erickson be inclined to talk about this at Dunham's local Presbyterian church, where the parishioners were known to support temperance rallies and lectures on uplifting topics? Erickson agreed and Lethbridge subsequently became the first community in Canada to commit to hosting a Chautauqua event. Local businessmen agreed to act as financial guarantors, and Erickson said he would provide trained staff to work with local people selling tickets.

Before bringing Chautauqua to Lethbridge, however, Erickson had to make the circuit commercially viable by lining up other Western Canadian venues. After obtaining commitments from the folks in Taber, Cayley, Nanton, and Fort Macleod, Erickson was set to begin operations. Alberta would become the first Canadian province to open its doors to a style of entertainment that had brought intimations of European culture to the rural communities of North America at the turn of the twentieth century.

Erickson was a farm boy from Wisconsin who first discovered Chautauqua while studying law at Stanford University in California during the years before World War I. He spent his summers travelling Chautauqua's West Coast circuit as a tent worker, and eventually became involved in managing and booking venues for the circuit. Erickson saw Canada as a potentially profitable entertainment market long before American radio, Hollywood, paperback novels, and television collectively generated a backlash and turned imported culture into a political hot potato for a country trying to acquire a sense of its identity. What would be viewed later as a manifestation of American cultural imperialism was seen in 1917 as a vehicle for drawing the isolated towns of Western Canada closer together.

Erickson's partner in the Canadian venture was twenty-five-year-old Nola Critz, a lawyer's daughter from Missouri who trained and worked as a college teacher before applying for a job as a children's storyteller with the Chautauqua shows. She met Erickson while both were working the California circuit. In January 1917 he asked her to come north with him and help establish a Chautauqua circuit in Western Canada. He offered her the challenge of signing up Regina, which—for reasons he never specified—he considered to be crucial to his success. "If Regina can be booked," he said, "then any town or city in Canada can be booked." Critz accepted the challenge and Regina became part of the new circuit. So did Saskatoon, Weyburn, Swift Current, Banff, Gleichen, Medicine Hat, Olds, Wetaskiwin, and other Prairie communities; a total of forty towns.

Calgary became the centre of operations for the new Canadian Chautauqua circuit. Erickson applied for Canadian citizenship because he believed a person had to be a Canadian to achieve success in Canada. He printed up letterheads bearing the name

Dominion Chautauquas. The featured artists and speakers for the first tour would include a number of prominent Canadian singers, actors, and musicians, as well as distinguished lecturers such as the Alberta farm leader Henry Wise Wood who would speak on political and military issues.

The circuit started in Colorado on 25 May 1917, and wound its way through Utah, Idaho, Oregon, and Washington before crossing the Canadian border. On 2 July, Gleichen became the first community in Alberta to welcome the sixty touring performers with their trademark brown tent. (The organizers chose the colour brown to distinguish Chautauqua from the travelling circuses with their big white tents.) The troupe criss-crossed the province by train and then carried on through Saskatchewan and Manitoba before ending up in Wyoming on 1 September.

The touring performers brought something for all ages and tastes. Before the program got underway, a children's parade marched through town. Other special presentations for children included puppet shows and clowns. The adults could hear Emmeline Pankhurst advance the suffragist cause from the Chautauqua platform; Private Harold Peat speak of his experiences "on the Western Front;" explorer Vilhjalmur Stefansson lecture on his Arctic expeditions. They could catch the exciting sounds of the Russian Cossack Chorus or the equally popular Hawaiian "dramatic and musical sensation," Waikiki Quintette. Alternatively, they could watch a popular melodrama such as *Smilin' Through* or *Peg O' My Heart*.

The venture was an immediate success. Chautauqua brought diversion, culture, laughter, fun, moral uplift, and education to cramped lives on the Prairies. Chautauqua offered many rural residents their first chance to hear a real violin as opposed to a homemade fiddle. Even the larger cities, which already had an abundance of music and vaudeville, welcomed Chautauqua as a pleasing addition to the cultural scene. The *Calgary Herald* held a contest for readers to provide their answers to the question, "What is Chautauqua?" Prizes in the form of Chautauqua tickets were given for the best answers.

The newspapers gave plenty of advance publicity to the tour and were effusive in their praise afterwards. The *Swift Current Sun* predicted the six-day festival would be "the greatest week of the year" and "worthwhile in every respect with its clean entertainment, inspiring music and instructive lectures." The *Lethbridge Herald* proclaimed its community "the Chautauqua town" because it had been the first in Canada to sign up for the circuit.

For Erickson, the bonus at the end of the first Canadian tour was the fact that Nola Crites agreed to be his wife. (Conscious of wartime anti-German sentiment in Canada, she had changed the spelling of her German-looking last name, Critz, to make it seem more like a British surname.) Their first home was a rented one-room apartment on the top floor of the six-storey Lougheed Building in downtown Calgary, four floors above the office that served as the Canadian headquarters for Chautauqua. Both Nola and John worked in the office. John looked after the general operations, which included managing a large army of travelling tent workers and local volunteers, and organized a winter season of short Chautauqua productions for presentation in community halls and schools after the big summer tent season was over. Nola handled the paperwork and bookings. She also developed a series of inspirational lectures, including one entitled "Highway to Happiness," which she presented as part of the Chautauqua programming.

The Ericksons ran Dominion Chautauquas from their Calgary office for eighteen years, developing a network of tent circuits from British Columbia to Quebec. It was generally a no-risk operation for them because leading citizens and local businesses underwrote the expenses and all the Ericksons had to do was supply the acts. However, they did suffer a major financial setback in the winter of 1918, after their second summer season in Canada, when because of the Spanish influenza outbreak, all public meetings were banned and public places and institutions were closed across Canada. The Dominion Chautauqua became one of the many casualties. Bouncing back was a challenge for the Ericksons because they had to pay all the travelling and hotel accommodation costs Chautauqua incurred before the 1918 winter season was cancelled. But, with the help of a $25,000 loan from the Canadian Bank of Commerce, they managed to turn the 1919 summer season into a paying proposition. That year, the six-day programs featured such attractions as an orchestra from Serbia and lecturers from Australia, China, and Japan.

Nola B. Erickson, dressed up to give her "Highway to Happiness" lecture: "Chautauqua was like a light coming into my life."

(GLENBOW ARCHIVES NA-1900-3)

The Ericksons settled easily into the Calgary community. They eventually bought a home in the upscale Scarboro district and became well known in the community for their volunteer activities. John was a Mason, a Rotarian, and a popular after-dinner speaker. Nola was involved with the YWCA, the Calgary Press Club, the American Women's Club, and various amateur theatrical projects. She was a co-founder, along with Edmonton drama pioneer Elizabeth Sterling Haynes, of the Drama League of Alberta, and she was a close friend of Nellie McClung, the pioneering advocate for women's rights. McClung once tried to persuade Nola to run for election to the Alberta legislature, even offering to act as her campaign manager, but Nola opted to confine her activities to the theatrical stage rather than venture onto the political one.

Chautauqua in Canada died in 1935, killed by the Depression, changing popular tastes, and the unwillingness of local communities to continue acting as financial backers. The Ericksons, who had both become naturalized Canadians, sold their Calgary home and moved to Glendale, California. It was tough for them to leave, they said, because for eighteen years they had provided what they felt was an important service to people far removed from the cultural advantages of major cities. The impact of the tent shows was summed up by one farm woman, isolated by Prairie winters and exhausted by overwork: "They kept me sane. Chautauqua was like a light coming into my life."

John Erickson became executive director of Glendale's Community Chest, a charitable agency, and worked on his golf game. He died of a heart attack in 1963 in his early eighties. Nola lived on in California for another two decades, still active in arts and drama organizations, and light years removed from the kind of world that existed when she first came to Calgary in 1917.

While the original Chautauqua has long been dead as a travelling institution, the name lives on in Canada and elsewhere, often associated with community recreations that hearken back to the popular entertainments of years gone by. Dozens of new Chautauqua performing groups have sprouted across North America in recent years, and a few Prairie communities (including Edson and Lloydminster) have adopted the Chautauqua name for their arts councils and farmers' market entertainment programs. Chautauqua's light still shines.

The Rainmaker of
Medicine Hat—May 1921

Charles Hatfield (centre) demonstrates his
rainmaking equipment to members of the
United Agricultural Association: "I will give you
a rainfall such as you have not seen in five, six,
seven or eight years."

THE FARMERS NEEDED rain. Southern Alberta's grasslands had turned into a dust bowl after many years of drought, and a rainmaker seemed like the best bet for salvation. The man for the job, the farmers decided, was Charles Mallory Hatfield, a California resident who, by all accounts, was one of the most successful drought breakers in the United States. Using a sorcerer's brew of chemicals in evaporating tanks installed atop six-metre wooden towers, the self-styled "Moisture Accelerator" was said to have brought rain to the sun-baked regions of California, New Mexico, Kansas, Oklahoma, and Texas.

The Lethbridge Board of Trade, however, was dubious. It asked the United States Weather Bureau and the Dominion Meteorological Office in Toronto to assess Hatfield's credentials, and received a thumbs-down rating from both. The board published the negative evaluations in newspapers throughout southern Alberta, and also circulated them in pamphlet form, warning settlers that if they wanted to spend thousands of dollars bringing moisture to parched lands, they should invest their money in irrigation, not in "a big lumber stand" with "some washing soda on the top."

Many of the settlers took the board's advice and looked at the irrigation option as a less risky alternative. The farmers of the Medicine Hat region, however, were located miles away from the established irrigation districts of southern Alberta and they decided to give the miracle worker a chance. They counted themselves fortunate when the man they called "Professor" Hatfield agreed to come to Medicine Hat in 1921, with a promise to "drench" the region with rain between 1 May and 1 August.

Hatfield had been in the rainmaking business for seventeen years when he came to the aid of the drought-stricken farmers of Medicine Hat. Born in Fort Scott, Kansas in 1875, he moved to San

Diego with his parents when he was ten years old, quit school after the ninth grade, and then became a salesman for the New Home Sewing Machine Company in Los Angeles. At the same time, he began reading books on meteorology, collecting rainfall data from the United States Weather Bureau, and experimenting in his kitchen with combinations of chemicals that, he claimed, could attract steam from a teakettle "just as a magnet draws steel."

By 1904, Hatfield was claiming positive results from his efforts to create rain in the Los Angeles area. Working with his younger brother Paul, then seventeen, he built a rain derrick in the brush country at La Crescenta, brewed his fumes for a week, chased away snooping intruders with a shotgun, and claimed victory when one inch of rain fell. Bemused local farmers said the smell from the evaporation tower was so bad "that it rains in self-defence." The weather bureau dismissed the suggestion that Hatfield had achieved anything extraordinary, saying that the rain was nothing more than a part of a larger storm system extending over most of southern California. However, the Los Angeles newspapers were impressed. They dubbed Hatfield the "wizard of the clouds" and reported that his "water factory" had proved successful nineteen times out of twenty when he was experimenting in the canyons north of the city. Thus reassured, Hatfield made an offer to the people of Los Angeles, guaranteeing at least eighteen inches of rain over a four-month period for a fee of one thousand dollars. Hatfield noted that the regular rainfall rarely exceeded eight to ten inches, and said he would accept no payment whatsoever should less than eighteen inches fall. The official weather forecaster for Los Angeles denounced Hatfield as a charlatan, but the newspapers said the young "rain engineer" should be given a chance. "Don't let it rain on the Rose Bowl parade," warned one editor jokingly.

Rose Bowl Day, 1 January 1905, remained dry for the annual street pageant and college football game, but the rains did start falling in Pasadena shortly after that. By mid-March 1905, Hatfield was just one-third of an inch short of his eighteen-inch target, and he still had a month and a half to go. He told reporters that his success was based on his ability to achieve "chemical affinity with the atmosphere." He did not "make" rain, he said, because that would be an "absurd" claim.

"I merely attract the clouds and they do the rest."

Hatfield's success in Los Angeles earned him his promised one thousand dollars in cash and countless thousands worth of publicity. Newspapers from California to London praised his achievement. "Genuine Hatfield Umbrellas" went on sale in Los Angeles at $2.50 to $4.50 apiece. Hatfield hit the lecture circuit with a presentation entitled, "How I Attract Moisture Laden Atmospheres." He told his listeners he planned to rid London of its fogs and to irrigate the Sahara Desert "as soon as the French government can be made to appreciate that I can really make rain." Neither of these opportunities materialized, but Hatfield did get a chance to prove himself again in 1906 when the Yukon territorial government invited him to produce water for the gold mining activities in the Dawson City area. For ten thousand dollars he agreed to generate enough rain to serve the hydraulic needs of the mining companies.

The Yukon experiment failed. Some rain fell but not enough to satisfy the mining operators. They terminated Hatfield's contract and paid him eleven hundred dollars in expense money. Undeterred, he returned to California, where he seemed to have better luck. Between 1906 and 1915 he landed dozens of commercial contracts and achieved what he claimed were uniformly good results.

His most spectacular result occurred in January 1916 during a drought in San Diego when Hatfield pledged to "fill the Moreno Reservoir to overflowing" for the sum of ten thousand dollars. Over the next month the rains fell continuously in San Diego, the reservoir dam collapsed, rail connections were washed out, streets were flooded, houses were destroyed, and fifty people drowned. A front-page cartoon in the *San Diego Union* newspaper showed an angry farmer with a pitchfork chasing Hatfield into the ocean. When he tried to collect his money, city council refused to honour the verbal contract. The city attorney said the deluge had resulted from "an act of God" and that if Hatfield wanted to press his claim for payment, he would have to sign a statement accepting responsibility for the flood and for the estimated $3.5 million in pending damage claims. Hatfield decided to cut his losses and abandon his quest for payment.

While the United States Weather Bureau tried to discredit

him by issuing rebuttal statements to any newspapers that printed pro-Hatfield stories, he continued to attract favourable publicity for his rainmaking activities. In Calgary a newspaper article, paraphrasing a laudatory account in an American paper, helped pave the way for his visit to Medicine Hat. Ignored in the article, however, was the fact that his previous Canadian venture in the Yukon had been a failure.

The rainmaker arrived in Medicine Hat on 20 April 1921. The sixty farmers who met him for lunch at the Corona Hotel thought it was a good omen when light showers accompanied his arrival. His contract with the United Agricultural Association called for him to produce four inches of rain for eight thousand dollars. "I will give you a rainfall such as you have not seen in five, six, seven or eight years," promised Hatfield. "I have never seen a country with more potential for rain production than this."

Hatfield set up his equipment at Chappice Lake, thirty-five kilometres northeast of the city. He worked in secrecy but a reporter for the *Medicine Hat News* was able to ferret out a few snippets of information. His towers, said the reporter, were not "as tall as those of Babel" but at twenty-five feet high, they were the tallest Hatfield had ever built and were designed to withstand winds of ninety miles an hour. The chemical tanks were made of galvanized iron, filled with what the reporter thought might be copper sulphate or silver iodide, and connected to the ground by copper wires that would carry electrical charges and generate cloud-like activity in the atmosphere. In this way, said the reporter, Hatfield could create an "artificial vortex or waterspout."

The first rain fell on 2 May, the day after Hatfield installed his apparatus. It was only a light shower, but it was a start. On the fourth day there was a heavy shower and on the fifth an all-night rain fell. Sightseers flocked to the area and a moviemaker named William Brennan came to shoot a film of the rainmaking operation. Hatfield refused to co-operate with him. He believed the filmmaker was trying to steal his secrets.

As each day passed more rain fell and precipitation records for the period began to shatter. The fields became so muddy that the farmers were unable to plant their crops. Hatfield received telegrams asking him to cease and desist. "Better take a vacation for ten days, giving us a chance to get our land seeded," said one wire. "Past eleven days had enough rain to do us for six weeks. Bring a shower every three days, preferably at night." Hatfield, however, saw the heavy rain as another success story. He publicized his "remarkable results" in a Sheridan, Wyoming newspaper. "Droughts, starvation, famine—they are needless," he wrote.

On 20 May, Alberta's provincial treasurer, C. R. Mitchell, visited the Medicine Hat area and announced, "The whole district is like an immense garden." The rains had stopped at that point. As the days and weeks went by and the dry weather set in, it looked as if the drought might be returning with a vengeance. By 25 June, the temperatures had soared to thirty-seven degrees Celsius and the crops had started to wither. The United Agricultural Association held an emergency meeting and demanded that Hatfield produce rain immediately. "There should be a good rain within a matter of days," he assured them. "Conditions are unusually poor for this time of year and I am having problems making contact with the clouds. Be patient."

It took another three weeks for the rain to arrive and there wasn't enough of it to salvage the wind-damaged crops. The farmers, realizing that they could be the victims of a boondoggle, warned that if Hatfield didn't make a better showing, there would be no eight thousand dollars. On 6 August, Hatfield met with the association executive and agreed to reduce his fee by $2,500. The total rainfall for the three-month contract period had, in fact, exceeded the promised four inches by a fraction, but Hatfield said the farmers deserved a discount because of the unsatisfactory crop results obtained. They asked him if he would come back the following summer for a return engagement, and Hatfield agreed. He told them he was not satisfied with the 1921 site and said that in 1922 he would locate his towers sixty miles northwest of the city for a better outcome.

Hatfield never did return. After he was gone a check of the weather records for Medicine Hat showed that in only nine of the thirty-seven years since 1884 had the rainfall been below four inches during the three-month contract period, and that the average for the period was 6.04 inches. The boondoggle was confirmed:

Hatfield had collected $5,500 for a rainfall that was more than 1.85 inches below normal!

Hatfield carried on with his rainmaking activities in the United States even as professional meteorologists demolished his "science" and branded him as a fraud. His failures began to outnumber his successes, but the public never got to hear about this because the newspapers only reported the triumphs. "Some think he is merely a great showman," said the *Los Angeles Times*. "But some, and always enough for his purposes, think him a man ahead of his time, who can do what the United States Weather Bureau and all modern science say is impossible."

The Great Depression finally put an end to Hatfield's rainmaking. Although he insisted he could reverse the ecological devastation in the Dust Bowl region of the south-central United States, he had no opportunity to put his claims to the test because there was no money available to hire him. When the depression ended, the modern technology of seeding clouds with silver iodide crystals replaced the arcane art of rainmaking, and Hatfield retired to Glendale, California to live on past glories. He died in January 1958, taking his secret rainmaking formula with him. The Calgary-based *Farm and Ranch Review* noted sardonically that the weather patterns in Medicine Hat had remained constant since his visit in 1921. "The rains still come about the same time each year, and the hot weather dries everything up at about the same time," said the periodical. "Maybe the Hatfield towers made a lasting impression on the skies."

Stampeding Circus
Elephants—August 1926

Runaway elephants trundle along Edmonton residential streets:
"Get out of my garden, you dirty beasts."

EDMONTON BECAME THE unlikely site of an African-style safari on a quiet Sunday afternoon in the summer of 1926, when fourteen circus elephants broke away from their handlers and rampaged through the downtown and west end. Happily for the runaways, this was one hunting expedition where no animals ended up hurt.

The excitement began at about 3 PM on 1 August, when the Sells-Floto Circus train pulled into town. With a crowd of three hundred looking on, the animal trainers marshalled elephants in the CPR train yards to haul wagonloads of circus equipment, lions, tigers, and chimpanzees from 109th Street to the Boyle Street playground on the eastern edge of downtown. The orderly proceedings turned to chaos, however, when a yapping terrier suddenly spooked the elephants and caused them to stampede. Led by a 1,800-kilogram elephant named Mary, they trumpeted westward along Jasper Avenue, tearing through gardens and vacant lots, trampling flowers and vegetables, and smashing fences to matchwood.

Edmontonians didn't know it at the time, but the Sells-Floto elephants had been causing similar trouble for quite a number of years. In 1908, a group of the animals had stampeded through Riverside, California and one of them, named Snyder, had trampled a woman to death. A dozen years later, Snyder went berserk again, this time in Salina, Kansas, and was shot to death by a group of cadets from the local military academy. Another rogue elephant, Charlie Ed, proved to be such a problem for his Sells-Floto trainers that the circus eventually sold him to the San Francisco Zoo where he gored a keeper to death and was put down by a firing squad of law enforcement officers.

In Edmonton, circus riders took to the streets with loaded rifles and iron bars when the fourteen elephants stampeded through the city toward the grounds of the General Hospital. Also taking up the chase were the police chief, Anthony Shute, and three of his offi-cers. (According to police records, they put thirty-six miles on their vehicle during the course of the afternoon's pursuit.) The hunting party quickly recaptured eight of the runaways. The other six ele-phants continued to rampage, smashing sidewalks and fences, and terrifying citizens, who ducked into school grounds and behind buildings as the elephants thundered past.

Not all the citizens were scared of the big beasts, however. The hunters were surprised to find one intrepid housewife standing defiantly in her front yard as three elephants charged toward her, wav-ing her apron and shouting, "Shoo! Shoo! Get out of my garden, you dirty beasts." The elephants separated as they passed her and, mirac-ulously, left the woman unharmed.

A few people suffered minor injuries as a result of the stam-pede. A six-year-old girl who was among the three hundred spectators at the train yard, fell and fractured her arm in the scramble when the elephants first escaped from their handlers. Also hurt was an elephant trainer named Curly Stewart, who herded Mary into a tennis court, and was trying to slam the gate shut when she turned and charged him. He grabbed one of her ears, but she shook him off, tossed him through the fence, and made good her escape. Stewart lost a few teeth and suffered bruising to his chest muscles, and later went to the hospital for treatment.

Mary remained at large while the hunters gradually rounded up the other runaways. Credit for capturing many of them went to a circus clown named "Poodles" Hannaford, who used loaves of bread as bait to entice the elephants out of gardens and keep them calm until the other circus workers could secure them with logging chains. In one instance, Hannaford shouted out the command, "Tail up," which is commonly used by circus trainers to make elephants link tails and trunks and parade around the ring in a circle. The bewil-dered animal raised its tail, Hannaford grabbed it with his arm, and the elephant marched solemnly back to captivity, doubtless under the impression that it was leading a procession of elephants.

Mary defied her pursuers for the rest of the Sunday evening. A night watchman at the Cushing Brothers' lumberyard was finishing his rounds at 11 PM when he was startled to see Mary smashing into his office. After causing a small amount of damage to office furniture and equipment ($35 worth, according to later estimates), Mary burst through a wall and spent the rest of the night wandering around a cemetery, loudly trumpeting her contempt for people who try to capture elephants. At one point, a policeman managed to rope her, but he made the mistake of getting too close to her, and she retaliated by tossing him over the fence into the graveyard.

It took an older and tamer elephant named Trilby—the matriarch of the herd—to finally bring Mary to heel, at five o'clock on the Monday morning. Trilby, who was more than one hundred years old, wrapped her trunk protectively around the younger elephant and gradually calmed her down. The trainers hobbled Mary's legs with a strap, chained her to Trilby, and Edmonton's great elephant hunt was over. The total damages amounted to a mere $110, according to police estimates.

Mary continued to create headaches for her trainers after the Sells-Floto Circus left Edmonton. Two years later, on 8 August 1928, the circus arrived in Lewiston, Idaho, where the temperature was close to forty degrees Celsius, and the elephants were grumpy because their water supply had run out. Mary decided not to wait around for the trainers to refill her water bucket and took off down the crowded Main Street, looking for her own water supply. Onlookers said she seemed to think the store windows were oases, because she smashed through several of them, scattering shards of glass and spreading panic throughout the business district.

Mary finally found the water she was seeking at a car wash where two residents were hosing down their vehicles. The residents fled screaming, Mary started drinking, and the trainers gingerly approached with chains at the ready to secure the runaway. Before they could contain her, however, they had to contend with the unexpected arrival of the mayor of Lewiston who brought his hunting rifle. He entered the car wash with the loaded gun, aimed the weapon at her head, and shot Mary to death. Her trunk was given to a private collector and a roadside plaque was later installed near the site of the old car wash to mark the demise of the wayward elephant: "She was only trying to find a drink of water!"

Revolutionaries
Elected to Town Council
—February 1933

Children demonstrating during the 1932 coal miners' strike in Blairmore:
"The most militant and best organized strike in labour history."

꧁꧂

ONE OF THE biggest funerals ever held in the Crowsnest Pass was for a 34-year-old miner named Joe Krkosky, killed in a colliery accident in October 1944 when struck by falling coal. The local Roman Catholic priest refused to attend the funeral because Krkosky was a communist, at odds with his Church and thus denied the right to be buried in consecrated ground. However, more than three thousand others —virtually the entire population of the Pass—joined the cortege as it wound its way through the streets of Blairmore toward the Protestant cemetery at the foot of Goat Mountain. The procession was led by the West Canadian Collieries band, followed by members of the United Mine Workers of America, representatives of the First Slovak Mutual Benefit Society of Canada, and three hundred automobiles. "Loved by all who knew him," said the inscription on Krkosky's tombstone.

Krkosky's importance to the coal-mining community was significant. For eleven years before his death he had served as a powerful trade union official and as a respected member of one of the most revolutionary town councils ever elected in Canada. While socialist municipal governments were elected in Cape Breton during the early 1920s, none wore the scarlet hue of the "workers' slate" elected in the Pass in 1933. "Blairmore has gone red," reported a correspondent for the *Daily Worker* newspaper after the unionized miners had taken their seats on council. "The communists are actually running the town."

While the *Daily Worker's* account was slightly exaggerated —the new mayor, for example, was not a communist—the new council was largely representative of a socialist working-class population that had lived and worked in the midst of poverty and labour unrest since the First World War. The labour troubles in Blairmore could be traced back to a miners' strike for higher wages in 1917 and another strike in 1919, after which the provincial government established a commission to look into the workings of the Alberta coal industry.

The commission heard terrible complaints from the miners about squalid living conditions, unsafe mines, poor sanitation, and inadequate schools.

The mine bosses denied responsibility for the deplorable conditions, and said they were doing everything their budgets would allow to improve matters. However, in reality, the conditions went from bad to worse. The commission's recommendations for improvements were never acted upon because, in the end, the Alberta government decided that the federal government—which controlled the province's natural resources between 1905 and 1930—should be held responsible. As a result, for the coal miners of Alberta the depression existed long before the Great Depression started in 1929. At that point the coal market hit rock bottom and the miners were lucky to get work one or two days a week for greatly reduced wages.

The Crowsnest Pass miners, frustrated by the inability of their American union to stop mine owners from imposing wage cuts, voted themselves out of the United Mine Workers of America and regrouped as the Mine Workers Union of Canada (MWUC). This was a hybrid organization, composed of political opposites. Its main pillars of support were conservative moderates on the one hand and militant left-wingers on the other.

Arguments between the left and right wings came to a head in 1932, when the conservative members were pushed aside and the MWUC became affiliated with the revolutionary Workers' Unity League, a national trade union federation backed by the Communist Party of Canada. Joe Krkosky, at age twenty-two, was elected local union secretary for Blairmore. The Canadian-born son of Czechoslovakian immigrants, he had been working in the collieries since he was sixteen and was characterized variously by his fellow workers as highly intelligent (his son would later become a Rhodes scholar), a rebel youth, class fighter, community leader, union militant, pragmatist, and peacemaker. While his schooling in Blairmore had been of a kind designed to turn the children of immigrants into "Canadians" (whatever that meant), Krkosky was viewed by the Czech community as being one of their own. His making had been their making.

Krkosky's election to the most important position on the

MWUC union executive was regarded as somewhat unusual for the time. The older, more established unions in the coalfields were not in the habit of electing twenty-two-year-olds to their executives. But Krkosky clearly had the right stuff and he handily defeated Charlie Drain, one of his colliery supervisors. (Drain complained afterwards that he only lost because the "Slovaks" wanted one of their own on the executive.)

As one of its first actions, the MWUC called for a general strike throughout the Pass to protest the imposition of wage cuts on the miners of southern Alberta. It began on 27 January 1932, with a series of wildcat walkouts in the Pass communities of Coleman, Blairmore, and Bellevue, and escalated into a full-blown strike of 750 miners after 1 April when all the agreements between the mine workers of the three communities and the mine owners expired. At that point the mine bosses characterized the work stoppage as a "red conspiracy" hatched by "communist agitators" from the Workers' Unity League in Toronto. But it was, in fact, a cumulative response to a series of local grievances. In Coleman, for example, the key issue in the strike was the refusal of the colliery management to distribute the work equally among all the miners.

By May 1932, the strike was being described in the local newspapers as "the most militant and best organized in labour history." On 1 May, the schools were closed at 10 AM so that the children could join their parents at a huge rally in Blairmore. Three days later, attempts by the colliery owners to reopen the Bellevue mine were thwarted when fifty would-be strikebreakers found themselves facing what the *Calgary Herald* described as a "formidable array of pickets," many of them women. Violence ensued, rocks were thrown, and "hand to hand scuffles took place between the RCMP constables and the members of the mob." More than a dozen strikers were arrested. The owners abandoned their attempts to reopen the mine.

The strike dragged on for seven months. When it was over, both sides claimed victory. The union said the strike had prevented further wage cuts. The employers said the strike gave them the opportunity to start removing the militant MWUC from the coalfields and replacing it with so-called "home locals" (in-house company-run unions) more to their liking.

The mine bosses blacklisted more than one hundred miners, and refused to hire them back because they allegedly committed atrocities against the companies during the strike. The companies, however, had always been eager to dispose of surplus miners, especially those they viewed as communist agitators, so there is some doubt about whether these alleged "atrocities" (damage done to company property) ever took place. All members of the Ukrainian Farmer-Labour organization were included in the blacklisted group, as were members of the First Slovak Mutual Benefit Society and Joe Krkosky, who, undaunted, continued his revolutionary work—this time as a political leader.

Five months after signing the agreement with the mine owners, the Mine Workers Union of Canada shifted its focus in the Pass from industrial action to political action. Its sponsorship of a "workers' slate" to run for municipal office and school board resulted in an overwhelming victory for the miners in Blairmore, including Joe Krkosky. Although the bourgeois Citizens' League tried to discredit the miners as communists (which some of them actually were) and as atheists (which most of them were not), the workers won every seat on town council and three of four seats on school board. (In Coleman, by contrast, the Citizens' League narrowly prevailed.) Ninety percent of the Blairmore electorate voted, including many "foreigners" who had never participated before. One eighty-year-old woman, Mrs. Rossi, unable to speak English, brought a lump of coal to the polling booth to show that she wanted to cast her vote for the miners.

The new regime proved more durable than the ephemeral administrations that were typical of radical movements in Canadian history. Krkosky served as a civic official for most of the next dozen years, and became a pillar of the community. In 1934, he won a seat on the school board with 540 votes. "The biggest vote ever accorded any candidate in the history of the town," reported the weekly *Blairmore Enterprise*. In 1937, he successfully fought off a final attempt by the old elite to rid Blairmore of the "communist menace" and was re-elected to both council and school board.

The workers' town council lived up to its name. It exposed the corruption of previous town councils, collected unpaid taxes from prominent citizens, and supported the efforts of the unemployed to obtain a higher level of relief from the province. It also refused to force those on relief to perform degrading "make-work" tasks, such as picking dandelions in school playgrounds and removing large rocks from unpaved roads. In 1932, May Day was proclaimed a civic holiday, and the town's main street was renamed "Tim Buck Boulevard" in honour of the imprisoned Canadian communist leader. When Buck visited Blairmore after his release from prison in 1934, another civic holiday was proclaimed. The "Tim Buck Baths" (in reality, two showers) were installed in a local school basement to provide bathing facilities beyond those available in the colliery wash houses. Blairmore also got its first public park, on a tract of land that became known as Red Square.

The workers' administration, which lasted more than ten years, could not solve the problems of the Great Depression. Nor could the MWUC. But between the two, they did give the miners a sense of dignity and self-worth, which had been missing from their lives in the past. And while the colliery owners tried hard to put the MWUC out of business, it was the miners themselves who eventually decided that the Canadian union should go. When several of the union's key Toronto-based backers moved to the United States in 1935, the Crowsnest Pass miners voted to rejoin the United Mine Workers of America and the Mine Workers Union of Canada passed out of existence.

Joe Krkosky, no longer blacklisted, returned to the collieries as a working miner in 1935, and also worked part-time for the United Mine Workers of America, trying to persuade the workers in the company-run "home locals" to shift their allegiance back to the union. After eight years in the mines, however, Krkosky decided he wanted out. In 1943 he attempted to move to a new line of work at an aircraft plant in Ontario. However, an order came from Ottawa saying that Canada's coal miners should remain "frozen" in their jobs for the sake of the country's war effort. Krkosky was not happy about this and responded by helping to organize a pithead strike to "study" the federal government's industrial relations policies. The strike was short-lived but it prompted a certain amount of national media attention. "The union still runs the town," said a CBC radio reporter. "And an enviable job they have made of it too."

On 1 November 1943, all the coal miners in the Pass went on

strike for higher wages. The federal government called the strike illegal, and threatened the strike leaders with sanctions, but to no avail. The mine bosses soon capitulated, agreed to reduce the work week to five days, and increased wages to the point where the lowest-paid labourers received $10.07 a day.

It was to be Joe Krkosky's last strike. He was killed in the mine a year later, on 11 October 1944, leaving a wife and young son. "He was ever keenly interested in all matters pertaining to the betterment of his district and of his fellow man," said the *Blairmore Enterprise*. "His place as such will be hard to fill."

At the time of Krkosky's death, the trade unionists still held sway in Blairmore with fifty-four percent of the popular vote, but the communist influence was starting to wane. Eventually, a more moderate administration would vote to eradicate Tim Buck's name from Blairmore's public places and quietly remove all signs suggesting a "red" presence in the community.

Warships of Ice—1943

༺ᐱ༻

ONE OF THE strangest Allied weapons plans of the Second World War was a scheme to build huge warships of ice to confront Hitler's U-boat menace in the Atlantic. It seems remarkable now that anyone ever took the idea seriously. But in wartime, ideas that might have seemed absurd under normal circumstances often enter the realm of possibility. Prime Minister Winston Churchill was convinced the ice-ship idea would work, as was Lord Louis Mountbatten, his chief of combined operations. And a team of Canadians actually brought the idea to fruition. Working in secret, they developed and built a scale model of the so-called "bergship," keeping it frozen in Alberta waters during the summer of 1943.

The ice-ship project was code-named "Habbakuk" after the Old Testament prophet (usually spelt "Habakkuk" in English) who foresaw wondrous works: "Look among the nations and see, wonder and be astounded. For I am doing a work in your days that you would not believe if told." Alberta's involvement in Habbakuk came to light in March 1946, when two Calgary men told the *Calgary Herald* they had played a major role in this "weird wartime scheme to build iceberg ships" for use as aircraft "stepping stones" in the battle of the Atlantic, and as mobile air bases for bombers in the invasion of Europe.

The Calgarians, both refrigeration mechanics, told the *Herald* they did not know the ice ship was part of the war effort when they were recruited in late 1942 to install air-cooling apparatus in the vessel. Because the Habbakuk project was top secret, only a handful of Canadian politicians, scientists, and engineers knew the real purpose of the work being done at remote Patricia Lake in the mountains near Jasper.

The bergship was the brainchild of Geoffrey Pyke, an English crackpot who worked as a "scientific adviser" to Mountbatten even though he had no formal scientific training. He got the job, apparently, because Mountbatten was in charge of developing new weapons and liked to surround himself with original thinkers. When Mountbatten learned that Pyke had devised several imaginative schemes for winning the war against Hitler, including a plan to use armoured snowmobiles for ground missions in northern Europe, he appointed Pyke to his staff as an ideas man. (The architect of the snowmobile plan was actually the inventor of the machine, Quebec's Jean-Armand Bombardier, but Pyke didn't tell this to Mountbatten.)

Pyke had developed an interest in the physical properties of ice after the *Titanic* disaster of 1912, when an international ice patrol tried in vain to destroy icebergs with explosives. After discovering that he could strengthen ice by adding wood pulp to water before it froze, Pyke submitted a proposal to Mountbatten for using this reinforced ice—which he named "pykrete"—in the construction of huge unsinkable aircraft carriers that would be impervious to bombs and torpedoes. Each ship would measure up to four thousand feet in length, and be hollowed out to carry aircraft. A ship would house up to two thousand crewmen in an insulated metal chamber, and be powered by two dozen electrically driven propellers to reach a top speed of about eight miles an hour.

The Pyke proposal, which ran to more than 230 pages, envisioned armadas of bergships launching fleets of bombers against enemy ports in Europe, and battalions of Allied troops coming along behind in ice landing craft shaped like Venetian gondolas. Although the memorandum read like science fiction (Pyke said afterwards that he conceived the plan while "resting" at a psychiatric hospital), the basic ideas were taken seriously by Mountbatten and then by Churchill. "Urgent action is needed," wrote Churchill in a memo to the British chiefs of staff in December 1942. "I attach the greatest importance to the prompt examination of these ideas."

Because ice was key to the plan, and because some people in England viewed Canada as a land of ice, the Canadian government was asked to undertake the necessary preliminary studies that might prove Habbakuk feasible. The head of the National Research Council, Chalmers Jack Mackenzie, dismissed the plan as "another of those mad, wild schemes" that could start with "a couple of crazy men in England, and get Churchill's attention and the attention of the highest people in Canada." But telling this to Churchill was another matter. Mackenzie had to co-operate. He put Canada's atomic research program on hold, and arranged for universities in Alberta, Saskatchewan, and Manitoba to begin stress testing ice. Larger-scale ice testing would be done at an outdoor location near Lake Louise, and a prototype of the bergship—measuring two percent of the immense size envisaged by Pyke, and made of ordinary ice rather than pykrete—would be constructed at Jasper National Park's Patricia Lake.

Work on the project began in January 1943. In March, Mountbatten dispatched Pyke and a fellow staff member, physicist J. D. Bernal, to Canada to check on progress. Mackenzie considered them an odd pair, and was particularly intrigued by Pyke's eccentricities. "All together he is a most unusual type and most people think he is absolutely mad," wrote Mackenzie in his diary. "Travelling with Pyke is like travelling with a small child. You turn around and he is not there. You worry that he is going to miss the train, and he finally turns up at the last moment." By the same token, Mackenzie did see something of the mad genius in the man. "He has moments of what amounts of intellectual intoxication when he is seized with his ideas."

The bergship model took about four months to build and it looked for all the world like a wooden boathouse mounted on a raft of ice, eighteen metres long by ten metres wide. Within this one thousand-tonne structure, an insulated wooden chamber held three motor-driven compressors that pumped cold air through pipes of galvanized iron to keep the ice from melting. Army carpenters at the Canadian National Railway shops in Jasper framed the hull. Conscientious objectors—Mennonites and Doukhobors who had not volunteered for active war service because of their religious beliefs—

were conscripted from a local labour camp to cut the ice for the base and walls of the vessel. When completed, the model was cut clear from the surrounding lake ice and anchored near the southwest shore of Patricia Lake.

Pyke and Bernal were impressed by the work. In a report to his English supervisors, Bernal said the testing had not revealed "any insuperable or unexpected difficulty in construction of the vessel." The next step therefore was to move from the testing stage to designing and building an actual bergship. The Montreal Engineering Company, assisted by two naval architects from England, was commissioned to do the feasibility study. The report was ready for Mackenzie by the time he visited England in May 1943, and it infused Pyke's visionary scheme with a hard dose of reality. Mackenzie told an obviously disappointed Mountbatten that the engineering design work would take at least one year, that building the first vessel would take another twelve months, and that construction costs for just one vessel would run to at least $100 million. One of Mountbatten's colleagues, a senior British naval officer, shook Mackenzie's hand and commented, "That's the first piece of common sense I've heard spoken about Habbakuk since this fool plan started."

At a subsequent meeting with Mountbatten and his advisers, Mackenzie exploded when Bernal insisted that all the major problems of Habbakuk had been solved and Pyke, who kept "grinning like an imbecile," just nodded in agreement. "I can't imagine such a situation happening in Canada," wrote Mackenzie in his diary. "Here we have a royal Prince with two mad advisers holding out against the entire weight of sound professional opinions of a country."

In June 1943, Mackenzie attended a meeting in London at Churchill's prime ministerial residence, 10 Downing Street. He told Churchill bluntly that it would be impossible to construct even one bergship before the spring of 1945. But Churchill wasn't willing to give up on Habbakuk quite yet. Because the battle of the Atlantic was now swinging in favour of the Allies, with convoy escorts disabling U-boats in greater numbers than ever before, and because new long-range bombers were eliminating the need for ice-ship air bases off the coast of northern Europe, Churchill thought there might be a role for Habbakuk to play in the war in the Pacific. He decided to pitch the idea to the Americans at a meeting with President F. D. Roosevelt and Prime Minister Mackenzie King in Quebec City in August 1943.

Arrangements were made to bring a block of ordinary ice and a block of pykrete to the Quebec conference, and a demonstration was staged that might have been conceived by the screen-writers for the satirical movie *Dr. Strangelove*. Mountbatten drew his revolver and began blasting away at the blocks. The ice shattered eas-ily but the bullet that struck the pykrete ricocheted. One version of the story has it that the wayward bullet then narrowly missed a British officer. Another says it nicked the leg of an American admiral. Either way, the demonstration seems to have failed to convince the Americans that Habbakuk was viable. Although they did announce at the time that they would become involved in the project, the Americans said later that construction of a full-sized vessel would only be possible through extraordinary effort and by stopping work on more essential wartime projects. "It has, therefore, been accordingly dropped."

The Patricia Lake model continued to be monitored for cooling and melting activity through the summer of 1943, after which the compressors were shut off and the ice allowed to melt. The metal pipes and waterlogged wooden structure sank to the bottom of the lake where they remained undisturbed until 1988, when the Alberta Underwater Archaeology Society received permission from park authorities to install a commemorative plaque and cairn on the lake bottom near the remains of the model. The inscription on the plaque encourages sport divers to respect Canada's under-water heritage.

In a final report on Habbakuk, Mackenzie said that the project had been technically feasible but far too expensive in terms of time, resources, and manpower. He predicted that the lessons learned from the project would serve Canada well in the future, when other uses for ice structures were found. And indeed Canada has benefited from the Habbakuk research in that it now uses reinforced ice for roads and aircraft runway construction in remote areas, and for off-shore drilling platforms in the Arctic.

As for Pyke, he never advised the likes of Mountbatten

and Churchill again. He moved from war to peace still full of ideas —including a plan for revamping the British Broadcasting Corporation—but unable to persuade anyone of their value. After he took his own life through an overdose of pills in 1948, the *Times of London* described him as "one of the most original if unrecognized figures of the present century."

"Last-Chance" Well Gives Leduc a Bonanza —February 1947

(YARDLEY JONES PORTFOLIO)

Yardley Jones cover-art sketch of Imperial Oil's Leduc Number One well blowing in, drawn by the artist for the book, *Last Chance Well* by Bea Hunter. Vern "Dryhole" Hunter is depicted at bottom right, wearing a hat: "I didn't think it would be such a big thing."

VERN HUNTER DIDN'T know it at the time but when he and his crew started drilling for oil in a frozen farmer's field near Leduc in November 1946, his bosses at Imperial Oil were about to throw in the towel. After exploring in Saskatchewan and Alberta for more than a decade, and after drilling 133 wildcat (speculative) wells without finding oil in commercial quantities (though it did find natural gas), Imperial was ready to start experimenting with an unproven method of converting natural gas to synthetic oil. Natural gas had limited commercial value then, because a pipeline hadn't yet been built to carry the gas to markets in central Canada and the United States. For Hunter, who would later take to using the nickname "Dryhole" because he drilled many of Imperial's commercially unsuccessful wells, Leduc was just another job. For Imperial Oil, Wildcat Number 134 would be Western Canada's "last-chance" well.

Hunter was forty-one years old and had been working in the oil patch for twenty-five years when he was hired as toolpush (drilling rig supervisor) on the Leduc project. Born in Nanton, the son of a Baptist minister who was paid more often in farm produce than in cash, Vern grew up believing that turnips and potatoes were the only vegetables in existence. He also believed, thanks to his father's teaching, that having any kind of fun on a Sunday—swimming, fishing, or playing sports—was a sin.

Hunter finished high school in Calgary at age sixteen and then applied for a job as a bank clerk. At the same time he applied for a job with Royalite Oil, a subsidiary of Imperial. The reply from Royalite arrived a few days before the one from the bank. "If it had been the other way round, I expect I would have been a banker," he said afterwards.

Hunter worked for three years as a junior clerk in Royalite's Calgary office and then was transferred to Turner Valley to do double duty as a clerk and truck driver. In 1927, when he was twenty, Hunter got his first job as a roughneck (drilling crew labourer) and married a young Calgary woman, Edwina Grant, whose pet name was Dean. They began their married life in an uninsulated tarpaper shack in a shantytown called Poverty Flats, on the outskirts of Turner Valley. Dean joked afterward that many of their subsequent homes were just as modest. She remembered in particular a converted power house in Bengough, Saskatchewan. "I just got the floor painted and curtains over the orange crates before it burned down."

Laid off during the first years of the Great Depression, Vern survived by digging ditches and chopping wood, while Dean sold eggs produced by their three hundred White Leghorn chickens. In 1935, Royalite rehired him as a driller, at ten dollars a day for a twelve-hour shift, with no days off, no paid vacation, and no sick time. He drilled several wildcat wells around southern Alberta and soon advanced to the position of toolpush. In 1940, he joined Royalite's parent company, Imperial. He was drilling near Brooks in 1942 when he caught the eye of Walker Taylor, the company's regional production manager for Western Canada. Taylor was on a pheasant shoot when he saw Hunter working at 4 AM trying to fix a malfunctioning diesel-drilling rig. "Don't you have a crew to look after that kind of work?" asked Taylor. Replied Hunter, "It's pretty hard to sleep when you've got an engine broken down." A few months later Taylor was appointed superintendent of the Canol Pipeline project—an ambitious and ultimately unsuccessful wartime initiative by the United States military to transport oil from Norman Wells in the Northwest Territories to Whitehorse in the Yukon—and he hired Hunter as his drilling supervisor.

Hunter liked to say he acquired his nickname, "Dryhole," during the three years he spent drilling dust in Saskatchewan between 1943 and the spring of 1946, though it's not something he would have boasted about at the time. At the end of that period, Imperial abruptly pulled its rigs out of Saskatchewan, claiming that the socialist CCF (Co-operative Commonwealth Federation) government wanted to take over the industry and expropriate the equipment. Hunter received orders to relocate to Provost, a few miles west of the Saskatchewan-Alberta border. After drilling what would be the last dry hole of his career, in Provost on 28 October 1946, Hunter was put in charge of the drilling crew at Leduc. Some of his Imperial bosses wanted to hire an American toolpush because of Hunter's long string of drilling failures, but Walker Taylor insisted that Hunter should get the job because of his dedication and commitment to hard work.

Hunter didn't think that Leduc would bring him any better luck. "Too close to Edmonton," he rationalized. He figured that fate would never give him a producing well just a few miles away from theatres, restaurants, and the home ice of the Edmonton Flyers, a Western Hockey League minor-pro team. Experience told him that oil was usually found in desolate locations, away from the trappings of civilization. Besides, the seismic data on the Leduc location revealed little to indicate oil or gas deposits in the vicinity. A geologist for Standard Oil of New Jersey, the American parent company of Imperial, was so sure no oil would be found that he announced he would drink any oil that flowed from the plains of central Alberta.

The drilling location was the Mike Turta farm, sixteen kilometres west of Leduc. It was a modest, ninety-seven-hectare spread with a couple of hogs, half a dozen cattle, a few chickens, and a horse. There was no tractor and no electricity and Turta had no mineral rights, so he wasn't about to get much oil money for farm improvements. Imperial offered him $250 a year for surface rights, plus twenty-five cents for every vehicle entering and leaving the farm.

Hunter offered to build a road around the homestead to the drill site, but Turta wouldn't hear of it. "Come through my yard," he said. Hunter tried to explain that the steady stream of noisy trucks would be very disruptive, but Turta said he would rather have that inconvenience than give up more of his cropland to the oil workers.

Hunter and his crew of four drillers and twenty-eight roughnecks spudded in (started drilling) the well on 20 November 1946. The rig engine operated round the clock in the cold for the next three months. The Turta family often invited the crew in for tea and snacks, but accepting such invitations could sometimes be risky. "Walking through Mike's yard was dangerous," explained Hunter, "with his ganders snapping at your heels like the hound dogs after Little Eva [in

Harriet Beecher Stowe's nineteenth century classic, *Uncle Tom's Cabin*]." The workers returned the favour by purchasing all their groceries from the Turta family.

Not all the neighbours were as welcoming as the Turtas. Drilling crews had a reputation for drinking and fighting, and the Leduc workers were as boisterous as any in the oil patch. They could never get service at the local hotel tavern or restaurant because they caused too much trouble. When Imperial threw a banquet for them in December 1946 to celebrate their safety record—a full year of drilling in different Alberta locations without a lost-time accident— the workers ruined the party by whooping it up like there was no tomorrow. At the end of the evening one worker had a broken arm either from falling over a chair or being thrown out the door (reports varied) and several others were the worse for wear.

The drilling was uneventful for the first couple of months. The crew hit a small pocket of natural gas at six hundred metres and then found a trace of oil, indicating that a marginally economic oil well might be possible. Hunter decided to go for broke and drill deeper, since the payoff from the work done to that point was so meagre that the well was hardly worth bringing in. Drilling deeper meant boring into a prehistoric sedimentary rock formation where the geologists believed no oil existed, but Hunter decided to see for himself what lay below.

At 1,500 metres, the drilling—to everyone's surprise—began to produce positive results. "We now knew we had a damn good well," said Hunter. "Yet we were getting these orders from Toronto to keep drilling and testing elsewhere." On 3 February 1947, a geyser shot 250 metres up the borehole, drenching one of the roughnecks in mud and light crude oil. Vern Hunter was "Dryhole" no more. "You could hear it like a train approaching when you put your ear to the pipe," he said afterwards.

For some members of the nomadic drilling crew, the discovery was anticlimactic. "We had become experts at abandoning dry holes and didn't know much about bringing them in," said Hunter. "Some of guys were actually disappointed when we hit Leduc Number One because it meant they were now going to have to stay in one place. A lot of them were young—they had been in the army or air force—and they would get tired of the girls in one town after a few months. They would want to move on and meet new ones."

Hunter's bosses at Imperial quickly grasped the importance of the strike. They urged him to name the day when he would bring in the well. Doing so in front of an invited audience of government ministers, dignitaries, and reporters would be an effective public relations coup for the company after all the dry years. Hunter was initially reluctant to do this because he knew how temperamental a wildcat well could be. "I named February 13 and started praying."

Word leaked out quickly and Edmonton radio stations began telling their listeners that something big was happening at Imperial's Leduc well. The tip-off occurred when the oil company ordered up catering from Edmonton's Cottage Tea Room.

Hunter spent the night of 12 February at the well site, helping his crew prepare for the big day. At about 8 AM the next day, he went home for breakfast and was just into his first egg when he received a call about trouble at the site. "It was a darn cold windy winter morning," he said, "and here we had a breakdown in the bloody machinery—it always happens." The men had been "swabbing" the well (using suction to draw oil to the surface) with a motor-driven pump when a shaft broke. "We had never used it because we never had to bring in wells before," said Hunter. "This piece of machinery must have been twenty-three years old."

The crew worked frantically all morning and into the afternoon as about five hundred onlookers gathered to watch the action. The well had been scheduled to start producing at 10 AM but there was still no oil by 3 PM. "When is it going to blow?" shouted one spectator as others in the crowd began drifting home disappointed.

Was Imperial about to fall flat again? Could this "last-chance" well really be just another dry hole? At about 4 PM, when most of the onlookers had gone home, the wellhead responded with a loud roar. "Here she comes," shouted one of the spectators who had stayed. "I think she's coming in now. Yes, it's OIL!"

Hunter gave the youngest roughneck on the crew, twenty-two-year-old Johnny Funk, the honour of "flaring" the well. Funk had practiced this the day before. He twirled a burning oil-soaked sack around his head like a lariat and tossed it toward the gusher.

With a mighty "Whoosh!" it erupted in flames and smoke. The flames shot fifteen metres into the air and a huge cloud of black smoke rose dozens of metres above that. "The most beautiful smoke ring you ever saw," said Hunter. He didn't know it at the time but the rising plume signalled the start of an economic expansion that would transform Alberta and increase the province's annual gross domestic product to $100 billion over the next fifty years. One of the first observers to recognize the well's potential was Calgary energy newsletter publisher Carl Nickle, who witnessed the flare and predicted in his *Daily Oil Bulletin* that the discovery would "blow the lid off" the industry. Canada, said Nickle, would go from being oil-poor to oil-rich.

Imperial threw a party in Edmonton's Hotel Macdonald that evening. Hunter, who hadn't slept much the night before, decided he was "too damn tired to go." He went home to bed because it seemed more inviting. "That day I learned never to predict again when an oil well would come in."

The Leduc discovery stimulated a tide of new exploration capital as geologists began hunting for oil in places they had once ignored. Within weeks of the discovery, central Alberta was bristling with oil derricks and suddenly Imperial could do no wrong. After the company drilled a second producing well at Leduc, the boom began in earnest. The flow was sufficient to convince Imperial that it should build Alberta's first oil processing plant on what is now known as Edmonton's Refinery Row.

The strikes at Leduc, and subsequent discoveries at other fields, brought significant economic and cultural changes to Alberta. Edmonton and Calgary went from being from small agricultural service centers to sophisticated cosmopolitan cities, centres of leading-edge scientific research and high finance, rich in theatre, music, art galleries, and intellectual life. Canada would eventually become the world's tenth-largest oil producing nation and, at 1.5 million barrels a day, one of the top three suppliers of oil to the United States—the world's largest consumer.

Leduc brought some changes to Hunter's life as well. After working as toolpush on Leduc Number Three—his last job as a rig boss—he was promoted to field superintendent for Leduc.

Promotions and other oil patch achievements followed, but Leduc Number One and the "Dryhole" nickname remained as his true passports to celebrity. "Although he might not have been Canada's best toolpush, there can be no doubt that he became Canada's best-known toolpush," said his second wife, Bea Hunter, whom Vern married in 1972. He appeared twice on CBC television's game show, *Front Page Challenge*. He was written up in English newspapers as the man who "single-handedly" drilled the famous well. His portrait appeared on an Edmonton bus pass. And a hotel in Nisku, just south of Edmonton, named its bar, "Dryhole Hunter's Lounge."

While Leduc brought him instant fame and years of media attention, Hunter said the historic importance of the discovery was lost upon him until years afterwards. "Hell, I was just a working man. I didn't think it would be such a big thing. But the people in Calgary and Toronto knew. A working stiff just does his job."

Calgary Wins First Grey
Cup—November 1948

(GLENBOW ARCHIVES NA-2864-13287a1)

Coach Les Lear, with eighteen-year-old running back Normie Kwong
at his left, holds the Grey Cup aloft as the Calgary Stampeders leave the
CPR station to start their victory parade.

THERE WOULD BE other Grey Cup wins for Calgary after the fabled one in 1948, when the Stampeders defeated the Ottawa Rough Riders and 250 white-hatted Calgarians cheered themselves hoarse at Toronto's Varsity Stadium. But none would be as sweet, as memorable, or as historically significant as that first victory in Toronto when the players wore leather helmets, and tickets to the event sold for $1.50 apiece. The 1948 Grey Cup marked the beginning of serious professional football in Canada and, perhaps more importantly, gave the nation a symbolic forum in which the conflicts between East and West could be played out. What might have been just another routine football final set the tone for what has since become an annual national shindig.

Like many other great moments in history, much of the 1948 event seemed insignificant at the time. Only later, when the rest of the country sat up and took notice, did Calgarians realize that something special had happened. There had been no grand plan; the whole thing just seemed to fall into place. Never before had a boisterous group of fans travelled by train for three days to see their team play in the Grey Cup.

The idea to accompany the team to Toronto began over a game of gin rummy at the Petroleum Club. A few of the members were drinking toasts to the Stampeders for having played the whole season without a single loss, and saying what a shame it would be if nobody was there to cheer them on now that they had made it to their first Grey Cup game. "Everybody should go down there," said member Bill Herron Jr., a wealthy oilman and rancher who had introduced the white cowboy hat to Calgary when he wore it in the Stampede parade a couple of years previously. "We should have cowboys, chuckwagons, horses, the whole shebang. Let them know where Calgary is. Show those Torontonians how

Calgarians like to let their hair down."

Herron and his colleagues had been responsible for the success of the Stampeder football team from the very beginning. They had raised the money that made it possible for a professional squad to be created in 1945, putting it together from the remnants of the Calgary Bronks, an amateur team that folded at the start of the Second World War. The salary scale for the new team was minimal; the Peanut Boys, as the Canadian players were called because of their low wages, made little more than streetcar fare. But the budget did allow for the football club to hire a top professional coach, Les Lear, who was one of the few Canadians ever to make a name for himself in the American National Football League. And the club was also able to recruit some top American players (known as imports) when a professional league in the United States, the All-American Conference, collapsed. Among the imports were two talented players from Honolulu—quarterback Keith Spaith and tackle John Aguirre—and pass receiver Woody Strode, a college football star from Los Angeles.

Spaith and Strode were a tightly coordinated toss-and-catch team that ran rings around the opposition. Lear was a coach who doubled as a player, and he often left the bench to help execute plays that proved to be pivotal in achieving victory. During the months leading up to the Grey Cup, the Stampeders won all twelve of the regular season games and maintained their no-loss record in the three games of the division finals. No wonder the card players at the Petroleum Club wanted to follow their team to the Grey Cup.

Herron and his colleagues decided that chartering a train would be the best way to get fans, horses, and chuckwagons to the Grey Cup. Herron brought along his horses and silver-studded saddles. The Buckhorn Ranch supplied the chuckwagons. Art West of the Canadian Pacific Railway lined up a thirteen-car passenger train. A baggage car became the nation's only rolling dance hall.

The unofficial leader of the Calgary contingent was Don Mackay, a popular radio announcer, city alderman, and future mayor, who suggested that everyone in the party should follow Herron's lead and dress in white hats and fancy western duds. Also in the group of

(GLENBOW ARCHIVES NA-2864-13288c1)

Calgary welcomes home its conquering heroes:
"They united Eastern and Western Canada into a strong bond
of understanding and good fellowship."

250 (later estimates boosted the number to five hundred) were a
country-and-western band and a few Sarcee (now Tsuu T'ina) Natives
in full traditional regalia. With the enthusiastic co-operation of the
band, Mackay organized impromptu square dances and singalongs
along the way. Whenever the train stopped for fuel, water, or a change
of crew, everyone on board piled out and danced in the station
waiting room.

The footballers didn't travel with the revellers. Coach Lear had them go to Toronto five days before the big game, and saw to it that they kept in shape along the way. Every time the train stopped, the players got out and ran from one end of the platform to the other. When the train arrived in Toronto, Lear spirited them out to the seclusion of Appleby College in Oakville, where he could keep them safe from the temptations of the big city. But that's not to say that the players lived like monks. "We trained hard and we drank hard," said Strode. "We drank rum and Scotch before practice just to stay warm. In fact, we had rum in our coffee at halftime. We used to say it was solely for medicinal purposes."

The Calgary football fans, who also liked their booze, attracted media publicity at every stop on the three-day train ride to Toronto. Newspaper and radio reporters relayed stories of their antics to towns and cities farther down the line. At Medicine Hat, the local mayor took part in a leg-wrestling match with one of the travellers. At Schreiber, Ontario, the group received thirty-six cases of beer in exchange for thirty minutes of square dancing and singing.

In later years, Mackay would say, "There were a thousand people to meet us in Regina, five thousand in Winnipeg, and ten thousand in Toronto." Actually, there were only a couple of hundred at Winnipeg, and nobody to greet them in Toronto except for a few bemused newspaper reporters. But the Calgarians put on a show anyhow, dancing jigs and reels on the platform at Union Station, singing the Stampeders' anthem—"Put On Your Red and White Sweater"— and holding up traffic as they wound their way across the street to the Royal York Hotel. The Ottawa Rough Riders arrived in Toronto at about the same time and nobody paid attention. The Calgarians had the stage to themselves.

The train was just one "Stampeder Special" that brought Calgary fans to Toronto. There was also a plane with twenty-one passengers. It too began life over drinks at the Petroleum Club. These fans almost didn't make it to the Grey Cup when they found they didn't have enough cash between them to charter a Trans-Canada Airlines (later Air Canada) DC-3. But the trip was saved when one member, Alex Bailey, pulled out his credit card. He was the only one in the entire club of wealthy oilmen who owned a credit card. Such were the times; credit cards were still a novelty.

Like the train travellers, the plane passengers got as boisterous as they could, even managing to attempt a mid-flight square dance in the plane's narrow aisle. When the plane stopped for fuel in Winnipeg, the pilot learned there were gale-force winds over the Great Lakes. Several passengers were bumped off to lighten the load and had to take the next regularly scheduled flight to Toronto. The group was thus separated, making it seem as if the wealthy oilmen from Calgary had actually chartered two planes.

The Calgarians and their supporters gave Toronto a taste of Stampede on Grey Cup Day, 27 November. They held a street dance in front of the Royal York. They cooked pancakes outside city hall. They paraded through the streets, on horses, in cars, and in trucks, with Toronto mayor Buck McCallum leading the parade on horseback. They even rode a horse through the lobby of the Royal York. Or so the story goes. At least three people were rumoured to have done so—Herron, Mackay, and footballer Strode.

While the Calgarians brought colour, energy, and excitement to parts of downtown Toronto, most Torontonians were not aware that anything unusual was going on. They had no reason to. For all the noise the Calgarians made, they had about as little impact on the average citizen as a convention of Shriners. One reason for this is that hardly anyone in 1948 cared much about the Grey Cup. As far as most football fans were concerned the big game in Canadian football was the inter-collegiate final played at Varsity Stadium the weekend before the Grey Cup. The *Montreal Star*'s sports editor came to Toronto for the college game but didn't bother to wait around to see Calgary play Ottawa. Nor did the CBC pay any attention. While a few private stations did consider the game important enough to cover, Canada's national broadcaster chose to play *Concert Favourites* and *Teen Beat* at the very moment that Canadian sport entered a new era.

The game saw Calgary gain the upper hand after two controversial plays. During the second quarter, with the Rough Riders leading by a single point, Calgary scored a touchdown after fooling Ottawa with a now-illegal move called a "sleeper play." Quarterback Spaith threw the ball to a player, Norm Hill, who had been lying unnoticed on the ground near the end zone after walking toward the sidelines as though leaving the field. With nobody around him, Hill easily made the touchdown. Then in the fourth quarter, with the Rough Riders holding a 7–6 lead, Strode picked up a fumbled ball at midfield and made his way toward the Ottawa goal line, hesitating often as if he expected the play to be called for offside. When he was caught from behind, Strode flipped the ball to Jim Mitchener, who continued on to the Rough Riders' ten-yard line. On the next snap, twenty-one-year-old halfback Pete Thodos stepped through the unsettled Ottawa defence for the touchdown that put Calgary ahead. For the next nine minutes—the longest nine minutes the team played all year—the Stampeders kept the frustrated Rough Riders at bay and held on for a 12–7 victory. Calgary had won its first Grey Cup.

Like conquering hordes the Calgarians in the stands descended on the field and within seconds they had torn down the wooden goalposts. They brought them back to the Royal York and set them up in the lobby, from which furniture and other breakables had been prudently removed. They then started a party that didn't end until the train arrived back in Calgary days later.

One Toronto reporter was perceptive enough to see that the game was likely the start of something big. "East is East and West is West, but Saturday the twain not only met—it congealed into one great roaring, pulsing, emotional mass of rugby-mad humanity," wrote Dorothy Howarth in the *Telegram*. "What statesmen at Royal Commissions and international conferences have failed to do since the days of Confederation, two handfuls of honest, hard-hitting, top-grade athletes did all in the short space of three hours. They united Eastern and Western Canada into a strong bond of understanding and good fellowship."

The Strode play was debated in the pubs and cafés of Toronto and Ottawa for weeks after the game. Should the referee have blown his whistle? If Strode really believed that the play was onside, why did he keep looking over his shoulder? "You never know what can happen in a game," said Strode. "But I looked at the ball on the ground and then I looked right in the mouth of the referee as I reached for it. He didn't blow the whistle so I just picked it up and ran."

The Calgary fans didn't care much about the agonizing of the Eastern fans. They had more than one reason to be happy. Before the game the Stampeders had been viewed as underdogs. The odds varied, but three to one in Ottawa's favour was said to be a standard bet. Perhaps it was just talk, or maybe the figures got boosted later, but there were reports that as much as $49,000 had been wagered by the Calgary oilmen. That meant they brought home more than a trophy, some shattered goalposts, and a lot of hangovers—they brought home a jackpot of $150,000 in gambling winnings.

Don Mackay was not one of the winners. He had already spent every dime he possessed just to get to the game. Whenever he wasn't cheering and charming Torontonians with his glad-handing, "howdy-pardner" style, he was wondering how he would feed himself on the train ride back home. He need not have worried. With the trophy in hand, everything started coming Calgary's way. Things started coming Mackay's way too. He had made such a name for himself on the trip that he became the candidate of choice when he ran for mayor the following year. In later years he would fall from grace because of his private use of city-owned cement. But in 1948 he was riding high.

The train journey home was a triumphal procession. Hundreds of well-wishers were waiting at the stations at Port Arthur and Fort William (now Thunder Bay) when the train rolled through at midnight. The Calgarians were presented with a supply of fresh fish from the Great Lakes, and from then on they dined in style. They were sleeping soundly when the train pulled into Kenora, Ontario at 7 AM but they didn't sleep for long. A local band marched through all the cars on the train to welcome the conquering heroes and their supporters.

It was the same all along the line. Farmers waved from their fields and factories blew their whistles. Townsfolk gathered at the stations and cheered. Children were released from school to welcome the champions. Small-town newspapers published special editions. Mayors declared civic holidays and provincial politicians issued proclamations.

When the train stopped at Broadview, Saskatchewan, a reporter asked Strode for his view of the controversial play. He spoke briefly and with little coherence. "Man, I'm full of anti-freeze," he said. He wasn't the only one feeling the glow. The Grey Cup victory stoked a fire in the soul of Calgary that was still smouldering forty years later, even though affection for the team had cooled considerably by then.

The Stampeders tried for a repeat victory in 1949 but were thwarted by the Montreal Alouettes. It wasn't until 1971 that the Stamps were able to put their name on the Grey Cup for a second time. But Calgarians were able to take some consolation from knowing that in 1948 they had changed the face of Canadian sport forever. They had put their city on the map and turned the Grey Cup game into a week-long national festival.

The Lonely Bachelors of "Dinosaur Valley" —February 1952

༰⚬༰

THE STORY CATAPULTED twenty single men to international fame, drew three thousand marriage proposals, and put the tiny Alberta hamlet of Dorothy on the world map. It appeared in *Parade* magazine, a weekend supplement in forty-five American newspapers with a combined circulation of twenty million. Under the headline, "Twenty Men Want Wives," it told how the male bachelors of Dorothy, a ranching community twenty-five kilometres southeast of Drumheller, desired to marry but were unable to do so because of a shortage of available women.

The story was written by Richard Harrington, a Toronto-based freelance journalist who initially pitched it to *Parade*'s New York editor as an article on what a cowboy does in winter. However, when the editor learned about Dorothy's "nest of eligible bachelors" he asked that Harrington change the thrust of the story to say that many of these ranchers lived on big spreads worth lots of money, and that they wanted to share their lives with wives and children. The story was published to coincide with that date in the leap year calendar—29 February—when young women traditionally claim the right to "pop the question."

Dorothy, named after the first white girl to be born in the district in the early 1900s, had once been a thriving little community, with a post office, three grain elevators, two churches, a grocery store, school, butcher shop, pool room, restaurant, gas station, and a population of about one hundred. However, by 1952 the population had declined to about sixty, and a third of those were single men who had come of age during the Second World War. Their fathers had brought wives with them from the old country, or went home to find brides after establishing themselves as homesteaders. But many of the sons missed out on matrimony because most of the girls raised in the district eventually migrated to the city. The only single women that ever came to the district were school teachers, and they seldom lasted more than one term before moving on.

The central character in the *Parade* magazine story was Tom Hodgson, a husky thirty-nine-year-old champion calf roper who was photographed removing his frozen-stiff laundry from a clothes line. "It sure is a man's world here," said Hodgson, the appointed spokesman for what writer Harrington called "the lonely bachelor fraternity of Dinosaur Valley . . . . Only sometimes some of us wish it was a little less so."

Hodgson lived with his widowed father in a forty-year-old ranch house that his father had built before the First World War. The house was rundown, as was the furniture, but Hodgson said he would be pleased to rectify this should the right woman enter his life. "Any one of us would be glad to build a new, modern house, with all the conveniences possible, if only we had a wife to give us the incentive." He added that while he and his bachelor friends had the will and the money to make life comfortable for a wife, "she'd nonetheless have to be something of the pioneer type, accustomed to long spells with no other company but her own folk."

Balanced against the loneliness of ranch life were such advantages as healthy outdoor living, clean air, and fresh produce from the farm. "For the girl with a yen for life on a ranch," said the magazine, "the field is wide open here in Dinosaur Valley."

The article brought instant fame to Dorothy and a slew of marriage proposals for the town's score of would-be husbands. The local postmistress—a rancher's wife who ran the business out of her kitchen—had to move into the barn to handle the sacks of mail that arrived by train three times a week. Hodgson received 1,814 letters in the first week. He also received sixteen telegrams and ten long-distance calls. He farmed the letters out in armfuls to his bachelor friends and they too were soon overwhelmed. "We bachelors aren't so badly off when you see how many lonely girls there are," said Hodgson.

The flood of letters turned into a deluge after wire services and newspapers in Canada, the United States, and Europe picked up the story. Many of the letters were addressed only to "Bachelors, Alberta." Hodgson, never much of a correspondent at the best of times, stacked the letters in an empty granary and tried to answer some of them. But he soon abandoned the effort.

The letters came from all over the world, some in languages the bachelors didn't understand. Many proposed marriage, sight unseen. British war widows said they wanted to leave behind the bleakness of post-war England. Divorced women in the States said they were seeking fathers for their children. Soviet factory workers offered to work hard on the ranch and asked for travel money "so you can try me out." More than half the letters said, "If you don't like me, please pass this on to one of the other bachelors." Hodgson was glad to oblige.

Some of the letters included snapshots of the women, in various stages of undress. A few included gifts, including a hot-water bottle and woollen long johns from a woman who wrote, "These will keep you warm until I get there." Hodgson was intrigued by one offer, from a woman who said she would pay his way to the States if he would stay with her and help run her car dealership. "You have to feel sorry for some of them," he said.

Parade magazine, sensing the ongoing commercial potential of what is known in the news business as a story with "legs," decided to make an American girl's dream come true by flying her out to Alberta to meet a prospective husband. The editor asked Hodgson to nominate a candidate, and he chose Rosie Mae Brewer, a Chicago machine operator. He liked the sincere tone of her letter, he said. In part she had written:

> You will probably have received a million letters
> like this, but I would like to correspond with you
> and hear about your ranch. I am twenty-eight,

unmarried, and I have brown hair and blue eyes. I live with my mother, go to school two nights a week, bowl one night a week, and work in a factory.

Accompanied by a *Parade* photographer, Brewer flew to Calgary (it was her first plane ride) in April 1952 en route to meet her dream beau. In Dorothy, parties were planned, the schoolhouse was decked out for a square dance, and the bachelors got busy ironing their best shirts. The entire community, including school children, turned out to greet her when Brewer arrived at the snowbound hamlet by car. "Hello Rosie," shouted the men. "Hello there, Bachelors," responded Brewer.

She spotted Hodgson right away. "You're taller than I thought you'd be," she said. "It's nice to see you," replied Hodgson. He accompanied her to the home of his married brother where she was to stay for the next three days.

Sixteen of the bachelors attended the welcoming party for Brewer. Too shy to speak, they just stood around until Brewer broke the ice by asking, "Is there a bachelor in the house?" They took turns dancing with her for the rest of the evening. She was the belle of the schoolhouse ball.

The next day, Hodgson took Brewer on a horseback tour of his 1,100-hectare ranch. He also took her for a ride in his Ford pickup truck along the frozen Red Deer River, and treated her to her first sleigh ride. He was impressed when she offered to help feed his chickens and cattle.

On the day of Brewer's departure all of Dorothy turned out again to say goodbye. The bachelors stood by waving while the *Parade* photographer shot pictures. Hodgson surprised everyone by kissing her on the lips. "I feel like I'm leaving my own family," said Brewer. "Everyone has been so kind to me. My life is lonely. I think it would be wonderful to be married and keep a good home for your man. I love to cook and I love children."

But the romance between Hodgson and Brewer never blossomed. Brewer went home to Chicago and married her steady boyfriend. (She admitted later that her loneliness plea was a sham and that her friends had dared her to write the letter.) Nor did any of the other bachelors find wives as a result of the *Parade* magazine publicity. But a few did establish pen-pal relationships.

Letters continued to trickle in for years after the event. By 1979, only seven of the original bachelors were left living in the area. Three of them had married local women, including one who finally shed his bachelor status at age fifty-nine.

Hodgson remained a bachelor for the rest of his life. Dorothy's population gradually declined as residents died or moved away, and eventually became a ghost town. The saga of the "Dinosaur Valley bachelors" is still talked about in the area, but for the most part it has faded into oblivion.

Calgarians Flee Mock Bomb Attack —September 1955

CITY PLANNERS CONCEIVED it as the largest civil defence exercise in Canadian history, if not in world history. They announced that in September of 1955, up to forty thousand Calgarians would be evacuated from the city and billeted in neighbouring towns as part of an air raid protection program called Operation Lifesaver. The object of the exercise was to see what problems would be involved in moving large numbers of civilians out of a threatened area in the event of a nuclear bomb attack. It was a time of armed peace and Calgarians had to be ready for possible aggression by the Soviets.

The man directing the Calgary exercise was Geoffrey Bell, a retired British army officer. Bell had seen active service in the two world wars and had run the civil defence program in Chesham, Buckinghamshire, where he also served on town council. In 1953, he took early retirement from the British civil service at age fifty-four and moved to Calgary, where he had family. Mayor Don Mackay, told about Bell's background, lured him out of retirement and offered him the job of full-time civil defence director for the city.

Mackay assigned Bell to develop a comprehensive defence plan for the Calgary target area. In the early 1950s, many had believed that the Soviets would save their limited supply of atomic weapons for American targets, and use cheaper incendiary bombs in the

Alberta "bowling alley" leading to the United States. But, fears of a nuclear attack heightened in the province after 1953 when the Soviets first tested the powerful hydrogen bomb. Civil defence planning in Alberta took on a new urgency, and mock attack exercises became the order of the day.

Bell's strategy for survival was to move the civilian population away from the line of fire before a bomb was dropped. This put him at odds with federal and provincial officials who maintained that constructing basement fallout shelters was the way to go. Bell insisted that mass evacuation was the only solution, and expressed his contempt both for the bomb shelters and for the ridiculous "duck and cover" American civil defence strategy, which envisaged school children hiding under their desks during an attack. "It will be better to look back on the bombed city from a safe billet in the countryside," said Bell, "than to gaze down from heaven onto the city with your corpse somewhere in it."

On 10 February 1955, Mayor Mackay told reporters that the Calgary evacuation exercise would take place on 21 September, a Wednesday, and that it would involve the entire northeast quadrant of the city. Bell had chosen a working day for the exercise, said Mackay, "so as to make it as realistic as possible." A similar withdrawal had occurred in Brockville, Ontario, the previous October, but it was on a much smaller scale, involving about fifty-seven hundred people. The Calgary evacuation would affect forty thousand.

The importance of the Calgary exercise became apparent when an official with the North Atlantic Treaty Organization (NATO) told the *Calgary Herald* that reports on the evacuation would be circulated to all member countries. "This is the first time in the world that anything like this has taken place," said Sir John Hodsoll, director of civil defence training for the United Kingdom. "It's a real genuine rehearsal where people will be doing exactly what they would under attack. That's why it is of particular interest to us in NATO."

The Calgary exercise became even more important when Vancouver cancelled plans to hold a similar exercise. "The eyes of all Canada, a lot of the United States, and some of England will be on Calgary," said Bell. "I'm going to ask the public not to treat this as an exercise in the sense in which we usually use that word, but as an actual operation of war."

The *Herald* was quick to stress the importance of the exercise. Editor Dick Sanburn, who had covered the Second World War as a correspondent for the paper, wrote in a front-page editorial that the "real" reason for Operation Lifesaver was the desire of "governments and their expert advisers" to ensure "there will be sufficient people left alive and healthy to breed and preserve the species" after a hydrogen bomb attack. In screaming capital letters and purple prose Sanburn spelled out the message three times in his column. At stake, he said, was nothing less than "the survival on this earth of the human species."

Others were not so inclined to buy into this kind of alarmist hysteria. Broadcaster Gordon Sinclair, writing in *Liberty* magazine, said, "we need civil defence about as much as we need leprosy." Medicine Hat mayor Harry Veiner called civil defence a "dead duck" advocated only by people "looking for cushy jobs." The Calgary *Albertan* newspaper accused Bell and his civil defence colleagues of being nothing more than a group of "fanatical volunteers" and dismissed Operation Lifesaver as a colossal waste of time and effort. Bell responded that it was "much better to be safe than sorry."

The *Herald,* during the months leading up to the test, repeatedly urged Calgarians to participate in the evacuation. "Experiment in the midst of a nuclear war is not possible," said the paper. "The citizens of northeast Calgary have the opportunity to show that they have a deep sense of the responsibilities of Canadian citizens by their co-operation with the civil defence officers."

Every house in northeast Calgary was assigned an evacuation destination in one of the outlying towns. When the air raid sirens sounded, every resident was supposed to pack clothing and enough food for twenty-four hours and follow colour-coded road signs along a designated exit route to the assigned destination. "Any attempt to disobey these instructions, and to substitute for them rules of your own making, can only result in the introduction of mob law with all its attendant evils," warned Bell. Pamphlets explaining the evacuation plan were delivered to every residence. Civil defence wardens gathered information from each household on the number of people in the household, the type of vehicles owned—if any—and details on any individuals who might not be able to travel due to illness. Bell assured the residents that the northeast area would be sealed off during the evacuation, municipal bus and trolley service to the area would be suspended, and extra police would be assigned to protect it from looting. Seventy officers would come from the city police department, thirty would come from the RCMP training college in Regina, and thirty more would come from the ranks of the city's recently formed auxiliary police force.

Seventeen rural towns were the designated reception centres for the evacuees. Pub owners from Airdrie to Penhold, and Irricana to Drumheller gleefully laid in extra supplies of liquor, anticipating their best day in years. "I imagine we'll be turning them away in droves," said one happy tavern operator. RCMP officers warned there would be no leniency granted if evacuees were caught driving home drunk.

The air raid sirens were supposed to sound at 10 AM on 21 September to signal the start of the evacuation. However, at 9:30 AM, Calgary radio stations announced that the exercise had been called off. Snow had been falling continuously throughout Calgary and the surrounding area since 11:30 AM the previous day, and the rural highways, not all of them paved, were in dreadful condition. The exercise was postponed for a week. "It was good sense to do this," said a *Calgary Herald* editorial. "The weather conditions were just plain filthy and the roads, at best, were hazardous." Some of the roads, said the *Herald,* "looked like battlefields." The newspaper's survey of northeast households suggested that participation in the exercise would not have been as high as Bell had hoped. More than fifty percent of those surveyed said they would not have taken part in the exercise, even if the weather had been perfect. "My husband has to work and I wouldn't go by myself," said one resident. Drumheller farmer Al DeBaer wondered what to do with the steer he had barbecued to make sandwiches for the Calgarians.

Rescheduling the exercise for 28 September brought a new set of headaches. Employers who had agreed to give time off to their employees on 21 September, balked at giving the workers another day off. Individuals who had made special arrangements to be free on the original date of the exercise, including ten civil defence wardens and several of the part-time auxiliary police officers, were unable to be free again on 28 September. Bell decided the exercise should proceed any-how, even though, as he said, "the state of enthusiasm has inevitably waned with the anticlimax."

The weather on 28 September wasn't much better. The snow was gone but it had been raining steadily and the temperature barely rose above freezing all day. However, Bell and his Cold War warriors were determined to soldier on. At 10:50 AM the sirens went off and Operation Lifesaver finally began. The imaginary hydrogen bomb, said Bell, was set to explode in mid-air above the north end of the Centre Street Bridge. He didn't say who would be dropping it (he didn't need to) but he did say it was just a "baby" H-bomb.

Bell directed the exercise from Calgary's civil defence com-mand centre, an underground bunker built for $70,000 under the clubhouse of the only municipal golf course that existed in the city at the time. (It was later named Shaganappi Point, when the city built additional courses.) The centre was constructed of concrete and steel, strong enough to withstand a near miss from a conventional bomb (though not a direct hit), and equipped with telephones and two-way radios to transmit instructions to civil defence officials in the field.

Perhaps predictably, things didn't go quite as planned. Most of the resident "refugees" ignored the air raid sirens. Some stayed at work, or went shopping, or stayed home and enjoyed a quiet day off. Of the forty thousand who were supposed to take a mid-week drive into the country, only about four thousand actually participated. Strathmore was supposed to welcome twenty-five hundred Calgarians, but only 299 showed up. Acme expected nine hundred and got ninety-seven. Beiseker braced for fifteen hundred and saw only 168. However, those who did go had an enjoyable time in the country. There was plenty of coffee and sandwiches for them —thousands and thousands of sandwiches, in fact. The travellers watched free movies in community halls and played bingo in hockey arenas. The few mishaps were minor. One person had a flat tire on a muddy road north of Calgary, and three cars were slightly damaged when they hit the ditch near Trochu.

All through the northeast quadrant the streets were silent. Police and reporters saw nobody on the sidewalks and nobody in the backyards—only a few dogs and cats. The only other mishap of

Operation Lifesaver occurred when a soldier was hurt setting off a smoke bomb that was supposed to provide an atmosphere of realism. Otherwise the evacuated area appeared like a ghost town. A fifteen-minute National Film Board documentary of the event showed nothing but empty streets, patrolled by police in cars and on motorcycles.

Most Calgarians knew the exercise had been a boondoggle, but Bell declared it a success. So did the *Herald*, though the newspaper did note that the low level of participation was "admittedly disappointing." The *Herald* had particular praise for the residents of the rural towns and villages. "They passed the test with flying colours, and Calgarians now know that they can count on the surrounding countryside for real help, if the need ever arises."

Though he faced some criticism from public officials, who questioned the value of emptying a city when atomic bombs were dropping, Bell continued to insist that Operation Lifesaver was a success. Over the next thirteen years, until he retired as civil defence director in 1968, Bell persisted in maintaining and polishing evacuation plans, doing his job as he saw it. After that, Bell devoted his time to volunteering with his church and with the Boy Scouts, and giving talks to school children about his experiences in the two world wars. "War is an imbecility," he told the children, "the kind I hope you will never have to experience."

Apathy would eventually become a chronic condition of the Cold War in Canada and elsewhere, and Operation Lifesaver would become just a distant memory. As superpower tensions waxed and waned in the decades that followed, most people eventually regarded the threat of global annihilation as an abstraction beyond their control and too horrible to contemplate. Civil defence organizations would shift their focus to natural disasters. Evacuation plans and air raid sirens would be abandoned. And Bell's once-celebrated civil defence command centre at the Shaganappi golf course—its evacuation map still pinned to the wall—would be kept as a parks storage facility until the city finally demolished the structure in 1997.

Watchdog Ousts Edmonton Mayor, Twice—1959, 1965

(EDMONTON ARCHIVES EA-10-696)

Official portraits of mayor and aldermen elected to
Edmonton City Council in 1964: "Politicians have no
business making money because of their office."

ED LEGER HAD no plans to get involved in municipal politics when he first moved to Edmonton in 1950. He was working as a federal immigration officer after a checkered career that included stints as an undercover police officer in British Columbia and as a special investigator with the Canadian army. His goal in Edmonton was to do well at his immigration job and support his family. However, when he was forced out of the immigration service in 1957, after a dispute with his bosses over his investigation of illegal immigrants, he found himself going down a road that would eventually take him to an aldermanic seat on city council, and a place in Edmonton civic history as a champion of honest government.

His journey to city hall began when Leger combined his $7,000 government pension money with his wife Ida's savings, obtained a bank loan, and bought the Southbend Motel on Edmonton's south side. A city hall employee told him that a parcel of city-owned property across the street from his new motel was zoned for industrial use, and therefore a competing motel could not be built. However, the land was subsequently rezoned without Leger's knowledge and a motel was, in fact, built. Leger wondered how this could have happened without a public hearing, and, after an examination of city hall records, discovered that his competitor was none other than the brother-in-law of Mayor William Hawrelak. Leger the ex-sleuth then went to work, probing the city hall records for other land transactions that might be questionable, and uncovered several suspicious cases.

In the fall of 1958, Leger presented city council with a 568-name petition demanding an investigation into the city's zoning practices. The petition accused Hawrelak of corruption, alleging that he used his position as mayor to make certain land transactions and business deals that directly benefited him, his family, and his associates. During his six years as mayor, Hawrelak had invested extensively in commercial properties that he either resold at a profit or used for hotel and apartment building. Caught up in the explosion of Edmonton's business growth after oil was discovered in nearby Leduc in 1947, Hawrelak seemed unaware that it was hardly ethical for the mayor to be operating as a land developer.

In January 1959, Premier Ernest Manning, at the request of Edmonton city council, turned the Hawrelak matter over to a judge, Marshall Porter of Calgary, for investigation. Porter delivered his findings on 9 September 1959, saying that Hawrelak was guilty of "gross misconduct" when he used his influence as mayor to have city property transferred to his brother-in-law for motel construction. Porter also ruled that Hawrelak acted improperly in five other land deals. At noon that same day the mayor resigned his office, issuing a press release that stated, "I categorically deny that there was any improper conduct on my part in regard to any of the matters under investigation or that I violated my oath of office." Two weeks later Ed Leger filed nomination papers for his first run for municipal office.

Leger ran on a platform of reforming the city planning department and changing public land sale policy so that it would no longer be possible for "a favoured individual to buy land at reduced prices and sell it for a great deal of profit." He won handily and spent his first two years on city council opposing the efforts of the new mayor, Elmer Roper, to push through a massive civic centre redevelopment that would have involved selling eighty acres of downtown Edmonton to an American consortium at fire-sale prices. Leger decided to challenge Roper on the issue in the 1961 mayoral race. While he lost the race, Leger did have the satisfaction of eventually seeing the civic centre scheme scrapped.

Leger abandoned his mayoral ambitions after his first unsuccessful bid, and bided his time until he could return to city hall as an alderman in 1963. At that point, he began developing a reputation for tenacity in the pursuit of truth and for ferreting out corruption in high places. City hall reporters loved his style. They saw him as a master of the five-sentence argument in which he raised all kinds of ominous possibilities and then sat back to enjoy the reaction. In the Leger vocabulary nothing was merely "bad." Everything was either "appalling," or "ignominious," or perhaps "asinine." He hated transients, cheaters of all kinds, experts, and excessive spending. But if anyone's personal rights were threatened by government encroachment, Leger would fight tooth and nail.

Hawrelak made his comeback as mayor in 1963 and soon found himself again in conflict with the watchdog whose scrutiny of city land deals had resulted in his previous fall from grace. In 1964, Leger launched his major offensive against the mayor. Hawrelak, he noted, had continued to buy and sell commercial properties during his four years out of office and again after he returned. Leger thought there was a potential conflict of interest there and called for a judicial inquiry into the mayor's land dealings. He was soon vindicated. The inquiry revealed that because Hawrelak held more than a twenty-five-percent interest in a company that sold land to the city for park use, he technically violated a section of the municipal act that would later be repealed. That minor infraction was enough to have Hawrelak disqualified from holding public office, and Leger and his council colleagues saw to it that Hawrelak was duly removed. In 1965, for the second time in his political career, Hawrelak left the mayor's chair under a cloud.

Although it might have seemed that Leger was making a career out of being the mayor's nemesis, he insisted there was nothing personal about it and added that he actually had a genuine respect for Hawrelak. Leger just didn't think it was right for a politician to be involved in conflicts of interest. "Everything else is open to negotiation, but not that," said Leger. "Politicians have no business making money because of their office. Unfortunately, people don't seem to take it that seriously these days. People are getting used to having politicians cheat and lie."

Leger continued to serve on city council while Hawrelak languished in the political wilderness, and when Hawrelak returned in 1974 for his seventh term in the mayor's chair, the two professed to be the closest of council allies. However, Hawrelak was only in office one year before dying of a heart attack. There were no further criticisms from Leger during this period because he had now adopted a practice of giving each newly elected mayor about a twelve-month grace period before starting to gather evidence of possible wrongdoing.

"Had Hawrelak lived, the romance would have ended," observed a fellow alderman. "The honeymoon period would have been over."

Five years after Hawrelak's death, Leger directed his sights at another Edmonton mayor, Cec Purves, whom he accused of being part owner of a company doing business with the city. Purves acknowledged his forty percent interest in the company, a parking lot maintenance firm, but denied any knowledge of contracts signed with the city. Leger insisted that the mayor should be removed from office because of conflict of interest, but the section of the municipal act that brought down Hawrelak under similar circumstances in 1965 had since been revoked. Council rejected Leger's motion that lawyers be hired to investigate the mayor's activities.

Leger continued to take on mayors and fellow aldermen as a kind of one-man vigilante committee during the remainder of his twenty-five-year tenure on city council. Asked why he remained on council so long, he replied, "I often ask myself the same thing. My wife has asked me to quit several times, but it seems that something always comes up around election time that makes me want to stay and fight."

At times, he struck observers as being little more than a perennial obstructionist. "He behaves like an automated doll that has been programmed to saying nothing but 'no' and do little but look for the bogeyman under the municipal bed," wrote political columnist Olive Elliott in the *Edmonton Journal*. But, at the same time, she noted that Leger was consistent in terms of supporting residents whose neighbourhoods were threatened by freeways or high-rises or parking lot developments.

In 1981, Leger claimed to have gathered enough incriminating evidence on "various misdeeds and mismanagement" to fill a "pretty good-sized suitcase." However, he never opened up the "suitcase" for inspection and often found himself in hot water because of his unsubstantiated accusations. In 1985, Mayor Laurence Decore launched a $50,000 lawsuit against him after Leger alleged that the mayor was "up to his ears" in patronage. Leger apologized and the suit was dropped. A year later, Leger finally lost an aldermanic race and Decore was exultant. "Oh, how sweet it's going to be," he said.

In January 1990, Leger died of bone cancer at age seventy-three. Some praised him as council's policeman, a valiant sentry who had guarded the public purse and kept civic bureaucracy in check. Others dismissed him as a publicity hound and a one-man kangaroo court. All—including a few former mayors and aldermen who had felt the sting of his accusations—agreed that city hall would have been a far duller place without the populist politics of Ed Leger.

Black Gold Mined from
Grit—September 1967

Construction workers completing their shift at the Great Canadian Oil
Sands plant, 1966: "The biggest gamble in oil patch history."

꧁

It rained hard in Fort McMurray on 25 September 1967, the day Great Canadian Oil Sands officially opened its plant for extracting oil from the Athabasca oil sands of northeastern Alberta. The smoke-belching barbecues had to be moved inside. When the smoke cleared, an eighty-five-year-old Philadelphia industrialist with a big stake in the venture stood up to put the significance of the plant opening into perspective.

J. Howard Pew, chairman of Sun Oil, had been sitting quietly and impassively at the head table, swaddled in a big blue overcoat with rimless glasses sliding down a generous nose, while politicians and other visiting dignitaries made grand speeches about resource development and energy self-sufficiency. When he rose to speak, the Sun Oil chairman surprised a few people by citing a Biblical reference. "In the Book of Genesis—the authorship of which is generally regarded as Moses—we find that God gave to man dominion over all of the Earth and then assigned to him the task of subduing it," said Pew. "It seems to me that the leader of the Alberta government must have had this injunction in mind when he commissioned our company to open up the Athabasca tar sands and thus make this great natural resource available to humankind."

Premier Ernest Manning, the Baptist preacher who was always careful not to bring his religious pulpit into the Alberta legislature, smiled when he heard Pew say those words. Manning recognized a kindred spirit in this doyen of the Sun Oil empire, a devout Presbyterian who had said, "We must be ready at all times to give a reason for the faith that is in us."

The Pew family had been looking at the Athabasca region as a potential oil source for more than two decades when they decided to take the plunge in 1967. J. Howard Pew had held to the single-minded belief during this period that if the North American

122

continent were to continue producing enough oil to meet its requirements, oil from the Athabasca area would have to play an important role.

In 1944, J. Howard's cousin, J. Edgar Pew, held preliminary discussions with a consortium of Canadian and British investors seeking funds for a plant to produce oil from what were then known as the Athabasca "tar sands." (Oil patch historians say the term was never accurate because tar is a synthetic substance and the Athabasca deposits contain a thick heavy oil called bitumen. They prefer the new and cleaner sounding name of "oil sands.")

J. Edgar opted not to involve Sun Oil in the tar sands project in 1944 because he felt the market conditions were not right yet. But J. Howard, who was then about to retire as Sun Oil president and who would stay on as chairman of the board for the next twenty-five years, thought that the company should keep its options open. Something had to be done, he said, to ensure the continuity of North America's petroleum energy supply and prevent the continent from becoming increasingly reliant on crude oil imported from Venezuela or the Persian Gulf.

As a young research scientist in 1904, J. Howard Pew had developed the first commercially successful petroleum asphalt (a product used for road making) for Sun Oil. He became particularly interested in the Athabasca region because its oil-laden sands had been used for road-paving projects in Western Canada after the First World War. When Alberta scientists ultimately concluded that the oil sands had more potential as a source of synthetic crude for use as feedstock in oil refineries than for road paving (because the paving projects were uneconomical), Pew continued to watch with interest. Sun, ranked as the twelfth-largest oil company in the United States, with revenues in the billions of dollars, had long been plagued with the problem of finding enough crude oil to feed its extensive refining and marketing operations. The Athabasca oil sands seemed to provide a possible solution.

In 1950, after years of testing and study, the Alberta government released a report saying the Athabasca oil sands were "entering the stage of possible commercial development." An Alberta Research Council scientist named Karl Clark had successfully developed and

Sun Oil chairman
J. Howard Pew:
"I am convinced
this venture will
succeed."

(SUNCOR ENERGY PHOTO)

tested a hot-water separation process for oil sands extraction, and experiments with cold-water separation had also shown positive results. In 1955, Pew decided that the time was right for Sun Oil to become involved. At his bidding, Sun bought a controlling interest in an Athabasca lease held by another American company, Abasand Oils. Abasand had been trying for twenty-five years to recover oil from the sands but was prevented by fire and other problems from making the venture commercially successful. Sun then struck a deal with Great Canadian Oil Sands, the corporate descendant of the Canadian and British consortium that had sought funding from Sun back in 1944. Sun granted Great Canadian the rights to mine and process the sands from the Athabasca lease (in return for royalty payments to Sun and Abasand) and undertook to purchase most of the output from a plant Great Canadian planned to build for the production of 31,500 barrels of synthetic crude per day.

In 1960, Great Canadian (today known as Suncor Energy) approached the Alberta government for permission to build the proposed production plant. Competing applications were submitted by Shell Canada and by a consortium led by Imperial Oil. Both sought approval for projects that would each generate one hundred thousand barrels per day; anything less, they said, would be uneconomical. But the Alberta Oil and Gas Conservation Board decided in favour of the smaller Great Canadian proposal because the board felt it was less likely to adversely affect the volatile market for conventional oil—oil obtained by the traditional method of drilling wells. The board was keenly aware that the old-time oil patch operators did not welcome trespassers on their hallowed ground. Edmonton oilmen dismissively referred to the oil sands as "poison ivy" and Calgary oilmen said they never wanted to see the "tar sands miners" darken the doors of the exclusive Petroleum Club.

In 1962, Great Canadian received the go-ahead to construct a commercial separation plant north of Fort McMurray. But money was now becoming a problem for the company. The initial 1960 estimate of $110 million for total capital investment had risen to $122 million two years later, and some of the key investors were pulling out. Even Sun Oil officials were having second thoughts about the whole project. Because the industry was then having difficulty marketing its oil, the Alberta government had established a policy limiting oil sands production to no more than five percent of the province's conventional oil output, and that—in the minds of some Sun executives—tied the company's hands and decreased the potential for profit.

It was finally left to J. Howard Pew—then eighty-two years old and still the undisputed captain of the Sun Oil ship—to make what would later be described as the "biggest gamble in oil patch history" and a "daring venture into an unknown field." First, he asked for a guarantee that the Alberta government would allow Great Canadian to increase its production rate from 31,500 to 45,000 barrels a day. When he received that assurance, in April 1964, he pledged to invest $67.5 million of Sun's money and arrange the rest of the financing for what was now to be a $190 million project. That meant spending a substantial sum on a mining venture where the technology was mostly untried, the operating costs were unknown, and the results were unpredictable. But Pew never faltered. "I am convinced this venture will succeed," he said, "and that it will be the means of opening up reserves that will meet the needs of the North American continent for generations to come."

By the time the Great Canadian plant opened on 25 September 1967—five days ahead of schedule—the cost of the project had escalated to more than a quarter of a billion dollars. That made it the largest private investment in Canada to that point. But if that seemed an exercise in folly, given the risky nature of the enterprise, the fact was lost amid the hyperbole and the barbecue smoke accompanying the opening ceremonies in Fort McMurray. Premier Manning described it as a "red letter day, not only for Canada but for all of North America. No other event in Canada's centennial year is more important or significant." Pew praised the "resourcefulness and ingenuity" of the scientists and engineers who had worked on the Great Canadian project, saying they had devised a "practical and commercial" means for producing oil from the sands.

As it turned out, the Great Canadian plant—which combined the features of an open-pit mine with elements of an oil refinery—proved to be somewhat less than practical and for many years something of a commercial disaster. Unforeseen technical problems, machinery breakdowns, explosions, and fires caused it to grind to a halt time and time again. The plant did not achieve its target output of 45,000 barrels a day until 1972 (the year after Pew died), by which time it had an accumulated financial deficit of $90 million.

But though it had more than its share of teething problems, the Great Canadian plant did pave the way for modern oil sands development. In 1978, when Syncrude Canada became the second large-scale commercial producer to start mining oil from the black sands, it was able to capitalize on the pioneering work done by Great Canadian and avoid some of the costlier mistakes. The excavation technology developed by Great Canadian, involving a system of draglines and bucket wheel scoops similar to steam shovels, remained the standard in the industry until the 1990s. The system was eventually replaced by a futuristic combination of satellite-guided mobile hydraulic shovels and the world's biggest dump trucks.

In 1979, the Canadian operations of Sun Oil were amalgamated with Great Canadian to form Suncor. That same year, when federal policy permitted the company to sell its oil at the world price of about US$20 a barrel rather than at the CDN $6.50 domestic rate for conventional crude set by Canadian price controls, the Great Canadian plant finally became a money-making asset for the company. J. Howard Pew would undoubtedly have felt vindicated.

A Tower Rises in
Calgary—June 1968

City engineers check the height of the new Calgary Tower:
"We need something bold and blood-stirring as a landmark."

THE "GOLDEN SPIRE," as Bill Milne envisaged it in 1963, was to be the tallest free-standing structure in the western hemisphere; a magnificent edifice to rival the great towers of the world; a beacon for tourists. Milne, then forty years old, was an architect from Winnipeg who had lived and worked in Calgary for thirteen years. He had a special interest in the kinds of structures that people built to celebrate significant or historical events, and he noted that they often reached for the sky. The Eiffel Tower and the Leaning Tower of Pisa were typical examples, as was the more recent example of the Space Needle, built in Seattle to celebrate the World Fair of 1962. Milne thought that Calgary should build something similar to celebrate Canada's centennial in 1967.

City council wanted to mark the centennial by building something "practical and sensible," such as an office block to house federal government departments. But Milne thought such an idea was lacking in imagination. "The government building proposal would be a good, motherhood type of thing, but it doesn't have any spark," he said. "We need something bold and blood-stirring as a landmark. We should celebrate a momentous time in a country's life by building something high." He sat down and made some notes on how a tower would work in Calgary.

The tower, Milne decided, should "catch the spirit of Calgary" and be a "focal point around which the city could revolve." It would be a "strong and significant architectural element rising out the downtown area, as well as being a self-supporting monument of dramatic proportions." Although built primarily just to be there, it would also serve a practical purpose as a tourist attraction, with a revolving restaurant and observation deck up top. It would complement the Stampede as a reason for visitors to come and spend time in Calgary. It would be twice as high as the twenty-storey Elveden House, then the tallest building in Calgary. The estimated price tag

129

would be $3.5 million. Anything less, said Milne, would be nothing more than a "penny-pinching" project.

Although the city fathers never warmed to the idea, other Calgarians loved the notion of having something unique built in their city. *Calgary Herald* columnist Lawrie Joslin predicted the tower would be an "exciting symbol for Calgarians, a new attraction of which we could all be as proud as Torontonians are of their unusual new city hall." (Toronto's CN Tower was not built until 1976.) Another *Herald* columnist, Johnny Hopkins, said the Calgary tower would be an "incredible splinter" and "the city's most exciting building."

The opponents seem to be in the minority as Milne developed his plans. However, the provincial government put a damper on the proceedings in late 1965 when it announced that it would not spend any money on what it called a "pylon restaurant" in Calgary. Then, city council formally registered its objection to the project by announcing that it would build a centennial planetarium (now the Calgary Science Centre) rather than a tower. That left a big question mark hanging over Milne's dream: Who would pay for it? Milne thought he had a solution. He suggested that the tower could be financed by selling twenty-dollar shares to all Calgarians who wanted a piece of the future. That idea never caught on, but corporate Calgary soon saw the tower as an opportunity for investment and self-promotion. Husky Oil put up most of the money, thus earning the right to put its name on the tower. The Canadian Pacific Railway supplied the two-block site, then occupied by its main passenger depot, east of the Palliser Hotel on Ninth Avenue at Centre Street. The CPR people announced that the train station would be demolished to make way for the tower, and that the redeveloped area around it would eventually include a parking garage, two office buildings, shops, movie theatres, and restaurants.

Milne initially had a substantial personal investment in the tower portion of the complex, as well as being its chief architect. He sent his plans and a model of the tower to the University of Michigan for earthquake testing and to the Imperial College of Science in London for wind tunnel tests. However, Canadian Pacific—operating through its real estate arm, Marathon Realty—wanted to put its own stamp on the project. It bought out Milne's interest and commissioned one of its own architects, Albert Dale, to see the project through to completion. Milne was naturally disappointed not to be involved any more, but he did agree that this was probably the best way to do it. He moved on to other dreams, helping develop other attractions for the city such as parks, river pathways, and a pedestrian bridge across the Bow River, and he played a major role in the creation of Kananaskis Country as a provincial outdoor recreation area.

Though the Husky Tower turned out to be somewhat plainer and not quite as bold in appearance as the space-age style "golden spire" envisaged by Milne, he was still happy to see it built. When the 190-metre structure was officially opened by the province on 29 June 1968, Premier Ernest Manning said, "There are many people you meet who you never remember because there's nothing distinctive about them. Cities are like people. Calgary will never be forgotten by visitors because of this distinctive tower." Milne echoed the sentiment. "I think it's a really good thing to have in Calgary," he said. "Many cities have high office buildings in them, but not many have a tower with an observation gallery that invites people up to look down over their city."

In 1971, Marathon acquired a controlling interest in the tower and renamed it the Calgary Tower. (The people at the airport continued to call it the Husky Tower because, as far as they were concerned, the air traffic control tower was the first and only Calgary tower.) A few years later, the first threat to the tower's dominance of the downtown skyline emerged when the Bank of Montreal announced plans to build a sixty-four-storey office block as a monument to Calgary's growing economic stature. The Calgary Tower would no longer stand in solitary splendour as the tallest kid in town. The bank officials said the new building would be fifty-five metres taller than the tower. It would have an unimpeded view of the downtown from the top and a picture-postcard view of the mountains to the west. But they didn't say anything about putting an observation deck in the penthouse so that citizens could enjoy these panoramic views.

The planned high-rise was never built. The bank's final

height was just forty-four storeys. But even if it had been built, it could never have attained the kind of international stature that the Calgary Tower did in 1988, when a gas-fired cauldron was installed on top to turn it into the world's tallest Olympic torch. By then the tower didn't even qualify as the largest building in Calgary, much less in the western hemisphere. The Petro-Canada Centre and the first Bankers Hall building had relegated it to fourth place in Calgary. But those late-arriving giants would never occupy pride of place in the hearts of Calgarians. As Milne observed, there might be room for many more tall buildings in a growing city like Calgary. "But only one of them can be a landmark. And I think the Calgary Tower will always be a landmark for people."

The Flying Manure
Bomber—April 1975

CAL CAVENDISH WAS a deeply troubled man when he climbed behind the controls of his rebuilt single-engine plane on a clear evening in April 1975 and told an air traffic controller he planned to "make like Louis Riel and rebel a little." He had just lost his pilot's licence after seeking psychiatric treatment for depression, and his career as a would-be country singer was going nowhere. He decided to register his frustration by staging a reckless publicity stunt. He would conduct what he later called "an aerial ballet" over downtown Calgary, showering the streets with barnyard manure and copies of his latest country-music single, a satirical song entitled "Government Inspected." Why manure? "It was a cowtown and I figured it could take a joke," said Cavendish.

He took off from the Springbank airport west of Calgary at 6 PM on Friday, 11 April 1975, after handing a note outlining his plan to a member of the ground crew. The radio in his Luscombe 8A wasn't working, so this was the last contact he had with anyone until he concluded his three-hour aerial drama. An air traffic controller phoned the RCMP, but there was little they could do but watch the drama unfold.

The escapade earned Cavendish the publicity he was seeking. The story was front-page news across Alberta. The coverage included information about his stalled musical career and excerpts from his lyrics as well a detailed account of the manure-bombing incident.

Born in Michigan, the flying country singer had moved to Alberta at age eighteen with his British army officer father and teacher mother. At that point he had been writing songs and playing guitar for eight years. He soon became what he called a "prideful prairie dweller" whose songs celebrated the joys of living in the Canadian West. He took up flying in his twenties and earned the nickname "Cornfield Cal" when the engine of his first aircraft failed and he was forced to land in a farmer's field.

Cavendish enjoyed some success as a songwriter and performer. He released four albums on small Canadian labels, and saw some of the singles land on the country-music charts. Country music star George Hamilton IV recorded his tune, "In the Mountains." The National Film Board made a documentary about him, *Cavendish Country*, which aired on CBC television. He performed his tribute song, "Good Old John," at a birthday party for former prime minister John Diefenbaker. CBC Radio used his song "Wild Rose Country" as the theme for a weekday noon-hour program heard across Alberta. (The network, Cavendish said, paid him just $125 for the song.) But he couldn't earn enough from music to make ends meet. He worked as a part-time security guard in between musical engagements.

In 1975, Cavendish was thirty-four and still struggling to find a market for his music. He decided to take a leaf from the publicity book of Stompin' Tom Connors, a Canadian country singer who resuscitated a faltering career after he displayed an intriguing message, "Stomp out Stompin' Tom," in big lettering on billboards around Toronto. When reporters discovered the identity of the mystery billboard advertiser, they learned he had been fired from several Ontario bars for kicking holes in the stage while performing. "How angry that man must have been," said Cavendish. "Stompin' Tom literally put his boot through the floor trying to get attention. My flying stunt was a condensed version of putting your foot through the floor."

The staff at the Springbank airport thought Cavendish was on a suicide mission when he took off from the runway, turned his plane around, and took a direct run at the tower. "We felt sure he was going to crash through the windows," said a controller. But Cavendish veered away from the tower at the last moment, barely missed hitting the roof of the airport manager's house, and then hedge-hopped toward Calgary along the Bow River, dipping under power lines as he went. When he reached the city limits he turned north toward the Calgary International Airport, still flying "just above the grass," buzzed the control tower, circled it twice, and then flew toward the city centre.

Shocked diners at the top of the Calgary Tower had to vacate the restaurant twice as Cavendish circled the structure, passing close enough "to see the faces and hands of the people inside." He also buzzed the Holy Cross hospital where his father was a patient, looped around downtown buildings at an altitude that would have allowed eighth-floor residents to look down on his plane, and then dropped his load of manure and records on the downtown streets. He used one hundred pounds of manure and one hundred records, he said, "to celebrate Calgary's centennial," and was careful not to release them all at once "because I didn't want to hurt anyone."

After three hours of daredevil flying, Cavendish began heading home to a rural community 420 kilometres east of Calgary. But he ran out of gasoline just north of Brooks and that forced him to land on a dirt road. He taxied the plane onto the parking lot of a potato-chip plant, and went to a nearby hotel tavern. After eating a ham sandwich and drinking a bottle of beer, he hitched a ride with two farmers to the Brooks airport, where he phoned his mother to say he had landed safely. He then turned himself over to the RCMP.

The police interviewed Cavendish for about three hours before releasing him, and said he appeared to be "a stable guy." A doctor at the Brooks hospital did a psychiatric evaluation and pronounced Cavendish "as sane as me." A Calgary pilot looked at the dirt road where Cavendish came down and said he had to be both skilled and lucky to make a safe landing in the dark. Because the plane had no lights, Cavendish would have seen neither the road nor the plane's air-speed indicator as he came down. Cavendish said he had flown for eleven years without incident and knew what he was doing. "I'm a very conscientious pilot," he said. "If they say I don't know how to fly, they don't know what they're talking about. That buzz-job on the Calgary Tower was a beaut." He insisted there was no risk involved. "It's more dangerous to drive down Macleod

Trail in a car than to do what I did."

Letters to the editor of the *Calgary Herald* both praised and damned the aerial rebel. Some said he should be celebrated as a colourful folk hero. Others suggested that the military should have shot him down. Cavendish said his "breach of civil etiquette" was meant to epitomize the bold and reckless spirit of the province. "Half of it was about the righteous indignation of Cal Cavendish," he said. "The other half was about the wild and woolly oil boom in Alberta."

Police charged Cavendish with two counts of operating an aircraft in a reckless manner, two counts of flying an aircraft at less than two thousand feet over an airport, one of flying too low over an urban area, and one of flying without a licence. "If they send me to jail, I'll start the best darn prison band you ever saw," declared Cavendish. The courts didn't send him to jail, but they did fine him three thousand dollars for reckless flying and suspended his pilot's licence for a further fourteen years. Judge Gary Cioni characterized Cavendish as a "bright man who has had his problems" and said his stunt should be viewed "with great seriousness."

The publicity did result in a few musical engagements for Cavendish—he played the Canmore Folk Festival as a headline performer and drew a full house to a concert at Calgary's 500-seat University Theatre—but not enough to advance his career to any great extent. After a few more years of struggling, Cavendish abandoned music entirely and became a long-distance trucker. He complained that the Americans didn't know how to market his "frost-bit" Canadian country music and that radio programmers in his own country treated him like a "backyard musician."

After driving truck for fifteen years, Cavendish briefly returned to the music business in 1994, renting Calgary's 2,700-seat Jubilee Auditorium for a comeback concert. It would have been more realistic for him to rent a community hall because less than two hundred showed up, but Cavendish didn't mind. He had spotted a sign in an Idaho gas station that read, "If it's going to be, it's up to me," and that convinced him to pursue his long-held ambition of performing in a concert hall. During the intermission, he invited the audience to participate in a paper airplane contest, using a model of the Calgary Tower ("my tower") as a target. The person who hit closest to the target won a dinner with Cavendish at the top of the tower and a flight with him over the downtown, featuring a "steep right turn around the tower—at a legal height." He had finally recovered his pilot's licence and owned his own plane again.

Cavendish told a *Calgary Herald* reporter that he had been a "pretty bitter boy" when he staged his bizarre aerial escapade in 1975. "I wasn't exactly a pyramid of mental stability then," he said. "I was pretty harum-scarum. But we mellow out as we go along. I'm fifty-three now, and I haul hazardous chemicals, nitrates or explosives, so I'm reasonably more stable."

Folk Festival Fever
—August 1980

Connie Kaldor strums guitar at the Travelling Folk
Festival and Goodtime Medicine Show:
"We were unable to remain a designated cultural
backwater any longer."

GOVERNMENT MONEY AND a rented school bus brought the folk music festival movement to Alberta in 1980. After a flurry of short-lived festival activity in the 1970s—most notably involving the small Edmonton-based Wild Rose Folk Fair, which ran for two summers before folding—the movement gained a secure foothold in the province in 1980 thanks to grants from the committee organizing Alberta's seventy-fifth birthday celebrations. The folk movement also owed a debt to Mitch Podolak, a former political activist from Toronto who founded the Winnipeg Folk Festival in 1974.

Podolak knew from experience that governments are always ready to loosen the purse strings for cultural events whenever there's an anniversary to be celebrated. In 1973, when Winnipeg was marking its one hundredth year as a city, Podolak applied for a grant to stage a centennial folk festival the following year and—much to his amazement—received $100,000. With that money he was able to book such top Canadian performers as Bruce Cockburn and Murray McLauchlan, along with such American stars as Leon Redbone and Bukka White, and establish a tradition that continues to this day. "I thought then that maybe we could go beyond one year, but it was only a vague hope," he said in 1999. "I never could have predicted the Winnipeg Folk Festival would still be around twenty-five years later."

After organizing three more festivals in Winnipeg and building it into the largest event of its kind in North America, Podolak moved to Vancouver and launched a folk festival there. He hoped to make a permanent home for himself in Vancouver, especially after the first festival turned out to be a winner. But he had a falling out with one of the co-organizers and within two years Podolak was back in Winnipeg looking for fresh fields to conquer.

Alberta was the next logical choice. The province already had a thriving folk club scene, with clubs in Calgary and Edmonton leading the way. The volunteer-run Calgary Folk Club, founded in 1972 and modelled after the clubs in Britain where bar service and audience conversation stopped when the performers played, had spawned a host of successful imitators in the city, including the Saturday Night Special and the Rocky Mountain Folk Club. In Edmonton a coffeehouse called The Hovel was a magnet for such emerging Canadian folk artists as Connie Kaldor, Bim (Roy Forbes), Ian Tamblyn, and Brent Titcomb.

In the fall of 1978, Podolak hooked up with Don Whalen, an Edmonton concert promoter, and asked municipal and provincial officials about the possibility of getting funding for an Edmonton folk festival. They came away not just with money for an Edmonton festival but also with $120,000 for a caravan of folksingers to tour the province for four weeks. Whalen agreed to look after the Edmonton event, while Podolak handled the touring show. The two ventures dovetailed nicely. Podolak made sure the Travelling Folk Festival and Goodtime Medicine Show, as he called it, would supply several of the artists and the sound system for the Edmonton festival.

Podolak assembled a troupe of Canadian and American artists including Sylvia Tyson, John Allan Cameron, Connie Kaldor, Jim Post, Stan Rogers, and Stringband. He rented a school bus for the tour, which took the group from Fort McMurray to High River. The performers were bemused by the school bus idea. One called it "an absurdity on wheels; a kind of demented high school outing for a cast of characters, the youngest of whom had left their school days far behind." However, the pay was good and many of the artists participated in the tour out of gratitude to Podolak, who had previously given them the opportunity to play the main stage at the Winnipeg festival.

There were no reporters on the bus tour so there are no media accounts of what it was like for forty-five people, including road crew, technicians, and backup musicians, to travel Alberta together for a month. However, we do know from later anecdotal accounts by the musicians that the tour started out with one of the headline performers—Stan Rogers—at odds with some of the others on the bus. Rogers felt particularly threatened by Jim Post, a Texas-born folksinger whose solo performances invariably drew encores and standing ovations. Even though Rogers was then on the verge of stardom, with ten years of professional experience under his belt and three acclaimed albums to his credit, he was still insecure around performers he felt were better than he. He dealt with his insecurities by getting into arguments with people. Rogers's other main antagonist on the bus was Sylvia Tyson. He had once told her pompously that, as a Canadian, she had no business performing in the United States. But she had struggled to establish herself in the States to survive as a performer, and didn't appreciate being told by this upstart newcomer that she should confine her activities to Canada.

However, whatever differences they might have had off stage were never apparent when they performed together. On stage, the Travelling Folk Festival artists were totally polished and professional. The only time Rogers came off looking like an amateur was when the troupe played High River, the hometown of MP Joe Clark, and Rogers made a lame joke about the former prime minister. "You've given us a prime minister," said Rogers. "Better luck next time." Half the audience walked out and the remainder reacted to his performance by sitting on their hands.

Rogers quickly learned from his mistake. By the time the troupe reached Edmonton in early August, he had elbowed his way to the top of the bill and was leading the cast nightly in the final singalong of the evening. Demonstrating all the characteristics of a performer now gaining self-confidence, Rogers chose for his final number not one of the standard festival closers, such as "Four Strong Winds" or "Will the Circle be Unbroken," but one of his own tunes, a rousing sea shanty called "Barrett's Privateers." The other performers struggled to keep up because they didn't know the words, but Rogers was in his element, bringing something unique and magical to the Edmonton stage. *Edmonton Journal* columnist Alan Kellogg wrote years later that Rogers did something important that night by putting his own stamp on the event. "It was an audacious, cocky thing to do, and entirely appropriate. The message was sent: Edmonton and the province of Alberta had served notice that we were unwilling to remain a designated cultural backwater any longer; that the test of any mature society included the songs, art, literature, dance and stagecraft of its people and guests."

Rogers was also the hit of the evening when the tour made its last stop, in Calgary at the end of August. The people in the crowd didn't know it then, but some of the Rogers songs they were hearing for the first time—"Fogarty's Cove," "Forty-five Years," "Mary Ellen Carter," "Northwest Passage," and "Field Behind the Plow"—would later become Canadian folk music classics. When Rogers died three years later, at age thirty-three in a fire aboard an Air Canada DC-9 in Cincinnati, many Albertans mourned.

The Calgary edition of the Travelling Folk Festival (nobody ever did figure out what the Goodtime Medicine Show part of the name actually meant) was sponsored in 1980 by the Calgary Folk Club, which bravely kept the festival going for several more years while dealing with constantly rainy weather, mounting debts, and dwindling crowds. Likewise in Edmonton, producer Whalen first battled the provincial government to get funding for a second festival and then kept it going for four more years before handing the reins over to broadcaster Holger Petersen. By the turn of the twenty-first century, the Edmonton festival, with Dublin-born impresario Terry Wickham at the helm, had grown to become the largest in Canada. The Calgary festival, co-produced by Wickham and Kerry Clarke, was in third place after Winnipeg and Vancouver. And Mitch Podolak, the bushy-bearded visionary who started it all, was back in Winnipeg running a non-profit cultural centre and dispensing long-distance advice and encouragement to folk music festivals all over North America.

Klein Becomes Mayor —October 1980

(GLENBOW ARCHIVES NA-2864-41620-35)

Ralph Klein, accompanied by campaign manager Rod Love (left),
extends condolences to defeated incumbent mayor Ross Alger:
"I felt the people were looking for a viable alternative."

To AN OUTSIDER at the time, Ralph Klein seemed like a political curiosity: a thirty-seven-year-old television reporter who suddenly got lucky, knocked off the incumbent mayor and the mayor's chief rival, and won what many people thought would surely be nothing more than a single term as mayor of Calgary. Who knew then that the roly-poly guy with the smiley-face grin would eventually go on to become the premier of Alberta?

Klein hadn't set his political sights particularly high (initially he just wanted to run for alderman) when he first decided in 1980 to leave reporting for politics. But he had told himself that if he ever made it to city hall, he would be there for more than one term. Once elected he would establish himself as the anti-establishment man of the people that Calgary needed, just as a former mayor, Rod Sykes, had done successfully for three terms during the 1970s.

Klein started unofficially running for council a year before he actually declared his candidacy. He did so during the course of his work as a journalist. Always concerned about civic affairs, he had covered city hall as a CFCN television reporter for ten years and during that time he often envisaged himself as an elected representative. "When you watch it for that long it grows on you," he said. At one point he applied for and received an appointment to the police commission. City council later rescinded the appointment when someone pointed out that having a working reporter on a committee dealing with the internal operations of the police force might not be such a smart idea.

Klein did serve during the 1970s on an urban affairs committee established to look after the needs of Natives migrating from the reserves to the city. And, as he admitted later, he functioned as an unelected one-man opposition when city council proposed in 1979 to build a $234 million civic centre complex to accommodate the growing office-space needs of an expanding city hall administration. Although Klein covered the story as a supposedly objective reporter, he never hid the fact that he strongly opposed the spending of tax money on what he viewed as a monument to civic bureaucracy. In one report he denounced a pro-civic centre propaganda campaign by revealing that actors were used in a city-sponsored television commercial showing derelicts eating out of garbage cans in a back alley near city hall. "I really couldn't present a balanced report because I thought everything that was happening was so wrong," Klein said afterwards. "I totally lost my objectivity because I felt so strongly about the story."

The staunchest supporter of the civic centre plan was the incumbent mayor, Ross Alger, a businessman and a patriot who had served his country as an RCAF flight lieutenant during the Second World War before serving his city as a school board trustee, chamber of commerce president, and alderman. Alger was already on shaky political ground before lending his support to the controversial civic centre project because council refused to back him when he tried to stall construction of a light rail transit system for Calgary. To add to his political woes, Alger became the perceived enemy of labour during a fifty-five-day strike by city outside workers, when he suggested that unionized municipal employees should be denied the right to strike. To compound this gaffe, Alger said in a television interview that he didn't see why the strikers felt they should be entitled to buy steaks or take trips to Hawaii or own colour television sets.

Calgary voters who shared Klein's concerns about the exorbitant cost of the civic centre project rejected the proposed expenditure in a plebiscite in November 1979. Undaunted, Alger said he would try to get the project approved when he ran again for mayor the following year. That made Klein see red. Every day after work he would repair to his favourite tavern at the rundown St. Louis Hotel near city hall and complain about Alger's refusal to let go of this expensive development project that Calgarians clearly didn't want or need. "I was mad," said Klein. "Then one day I just decided to do something about it and run for mayor. Nobody suggested it to me. Everyone thought I was absolutely crazy."

But Klein didn't think he was crazy. He saw that Alger was vulnerable and thought he had a good chance of defeating him. "I felt that Alger, even though he was a very nice man, had really lost touch with the people. He was more of an accountant and administrator, as opposed to a person who was out there in the community. I felt the people were looking for a viable alternative. I felt that if one could present oneself properly and talk intelligently about the issues and create a feeling that one knew as much about city hall as anyone else, perhaps a lot more, that there would be a pretty good chance of winning."

There was a second declared mayoral candidate, Alderman Peter Petrasuk. Klein viewed him as suspect because he was a lawyer representing some of the landowners who stood to profit from the city's purchase of three downtown blocks for the new civic centre. There was also a third potential candidate, University of Calgary professor Phil Elder, but Klein didn't think he had much chance of winning either because Elder had already painted himself into a loser's corner by running unsuccessfully for alderman as a left-wing reformer in 1977. The only viable candidate, as Klein saw it, was Klein himself.

City hall observers agreed that Alger was, in the words of former mayor Sykes, a "dead duck," and predicted that he would lose the race because of his grandiose spending plans. But they also assumed that there would be some kind of orderly succession with Petrasuk, or one of the other aldermen, taking over as mayor. Nobody thought for a moment that a maverick outsider like Klein would jump in and seize the throne.

The only people to take Klein seriously in the beginning were his wife Colleen and a couple of lawyer friends who felt Calgary needed a mayor with a common touch. His colleagues at CFCN laughed him out of the office when Klein announced in August 1980 that he was planning to run. Even his father Phil shook his head and asked Ralph if he were serious. But Phil did give Ralph some money and the use of his camper for a campaign vehicle. And the *Calgary Herald* did print what editor-in-chief Bill Gold then vowed would be the first and last story about Ralph Klein's candidacy to appear on the front page of the paper. (In the process the *Herald* scooped CFCN, which ignored the news about its own reporter.)

With less than $300 in his election coffers, Klein ran his campaign on the cheap, appearing at town hall meetings and pledging to make city hall more open and accessible. While Alger and Petrasuk were talking growth strategies and fiscal responsibility, Klein was promising to fix potholes and listen to the folks. Soon the media began to sit up and take notice. After one community forum, a *Herald* columnist, Merv Anderson, called Klein aside and said, "You're really serious about this, aren't you?" "Of course I am," replied Klein. Anderson went back to the paper and wrote a column saying that Klein was a contender.

The Klein campaign received its next boost when Rod Love came aboard. He was a twenty-seven-year-old political science student at the University of Calgary who paid for his living expenses by waiting on tables at the Keg 'n' Cleaver steak restaurant downtown. He wanted to put his political theories to the test, and first he offered his services as a strategist to both Alger and then Petrasuk. When they told him they were not interested, he visited Klein at his campaign office, located next to a demolition site across the road from the St. Louis Hotel. Klein was in the office by himself, counting out the dollar bills and coins that made up his modest war chest. Love asked if he could help, and Klein immediately put him to work as a driver, piloting his father's camper through the streets of downtown Calgary to a meeting with a businessman who had offered to provide Klein with better office space. When Love looked over his shoulder, he saw the grinning mayoral candidate standing at the back of the moving camper, stripped to his underwear, changing into his only suit, with a Bacardi rum and Coke in one hand and a Players Extra Light cigarette in the other. For a moment Love wondered whether a career at the Keg might not be his best bet after all.

Love's campaign strategy was to target the parts of the city where Klein's kind of people—the non–chamber of commerce types who went to the football games and the beer parlours—might deliver a strong vote. "Identify your market and saturate it," said Love. "Forget the areas where Alger has his support. You're not going to get any votes out of there. That's what coming up the middle is all about. You go where you know you're strong and you take your chances with the undecided [voters]."

Klein also picked up some tips from a former television anchorman in Spokane, Ron Bair, who had made a successful run for the mayor's chair in his city without spending a lot of money. "I watched him on TV and thought it would be a good idea to pick his brains," said Klein. Bair advised Klein not to make any specific promises apart from a pledge to be accountable to the voters. For the most part, Klein took his advice. However, he did make some promises that later came back to haunt him. One was a pledge to stop the northwest leg of the light rail transit system from bulldozing through the inner-city community of Hillhurst-Sunnyside. Another was a promise not to spend tax money on anything remotely resembling the lavish civic centre complex that Alger supported. Both projects eventually went through, more or less as the city administration had intended. Klein would discover after he was elected that the mayor was simply powerless to reverse civic projects already under way. (Alger would note ruefully that the replacement civic centre was only slightly less grandiose than the one that cost him the election.)

As the election momentum picked up, Klein managed to raise $29,000 for a campaign that ended up costing him $35,000. (One post-election fundraising dinner took care of the $6,000 shortfall.) His supporters included his beer-drinking buddies from the St. Louis, a few disenchanted civic employees, and several total strangers who simply phoned him up and told him they wanted an alternative to the chamber of commerce gang at city hall. When the race was over, the chamber of commerce gang was out, the beer parlour guys were in, and city hall was changed forever. "It was as if we both went home and wrote the perfect script for ourselves," said Love. "Ralph went from covering city hall to running it, and I went from [studying] political science to about the number one political job in town." as the new mayor's executive assistant.

With a last-minute vote of confidence from former mayor Sykes in his pocket, Klein rode to victory on 15 October 1980, with 44.5 percent of the popular vote (64,849 to Alger's 49,832 and Petrasuk's 27,040). For the next three years he had to work hard to prove he had something going for him other than simply the desire to be a "people's mayor." The business establishment regarded him as a flake and a fluke and thought he would be gone after the next election. They thought this especially in 1982, when Klein gained national attention with his "bums and creeps" line about the kinds of easterners he didn't want moving to Calgary during the oil boom. At first it seemed like a major gaffe and Klein had to hastily organize a fence-mending tour of eastern Canada to explain what he meant. But the tour was a public relations coup, Klein came home to a folk hero's welcome, and later he used the incident to comic advantage in speeches to visiting conventioneers. "Those of you from east of the Manitoba border are especially welcome," he told a group of Kinsmen at a fundraising dinner. "You're welcome as long as you check your guns and don't rob our banks."

By the time Klein ran for re-election in 1983, he was ready to take on anyone who viewed him as just a one-term wonder with a reputation for partying and losing his temper in front of the television cameras. He had spent three years keeping the lines of communication open at city hall, going out to the communities, telling people what was planned for their neighbourhoods in terms of improvements and infrastructure changes (something the previous administrations had never done), and, most importantly, giving them the straight goods about Calgary's mounting municipal debt. "Everything has a price," he said when the debt reached $1.6 billion, up from $659 million in 1980.

In the 1983 mayoral election, Klein defeated Alderman Sue Higgins, who tried to make civic spending the key issue. He also ran for and won the 1986 election on the debt issue. After that came the lavish civic expenditures associated with the 1988 Winter Olympics and then, in March 1989, Klein's leap from municipal to provincial politics. The future premier, who would become known for budget slashing rather than big spending, was on his way.

Notley Plane Crash Survivors—October 1984

❧

THE BIG NEWS in the Alberta newspapers on 20 October 1984 was that provincial New Democrat leader Grant Notley had died along with five others in a plane crash near High Prairie. He had devoted twenty-two years to making the New Democrats a credible force in Alberta politics, and he died at a time when political observers believed his party was about to make a major breakthrough.

Notley's death, at age forty-five, came as a great shock to Albertans. Much of the newspaper coverage, as one would expect, was devoted to lamenting his loss. Less coverage was given to the deaths of the five others, and to the fact that four passengers, including provincial housing minister Larry Shaben, survived the crash of the twin-engine Wapiti Aviation plane. Virtually no coverage was given, at least in the big-city newspapers, to the fact that there also was a hero in this story. Three of the passengers survived because of the rescue efforts and bush survival skills of twenty-seven-year-old prisoner Paul Archambault, who was being escorted by an RCMP officer to face charges in Grande Prairie.

Archambault was a drifter from Ottawa who dropped out of school at age sixteen and then wandered back and forth across the country, picking up casual work as he went. In Grande Prairie, where he lived in a small apartment on the upper floor of a two-storey office building, he worked as an automobile mechanic until he was fired for showing up late. He mislaid his keys after a night of drinking in

August 1984, broke an office window to get upstairs into his apartment, and was subsequently charged with public mischief. He failed to make the court date, skipped town, and was arrested two months later in Kamloops, British Columbia. He spent five days in custody at the Edmonton Remand Centre before being transferred to Grande Prairie.

RCMP constable Scott Deschamps was the officer assigned to escort Archambault from Edmonton to Grande Prairie via High Prairie. After talking to the prisoner for a few hours at the Edmonton Remand Centre and then at the airport, Deschamps decided to remove his handcuffs before they boarded the Piper Navajo Chieftain aircraft. "I felt he posed no threat to me," Deschamps explained afterwards. That decision helped save both their lives.

The crash occurred as the plane was approaching the High Prairie airport in dense fog at about 8:30 PM. The plane, flying at the low altitude of eight hundred feet, slammed into trees on a hillside about thirty kilometres from the airport, and ploughed through the bush for several metres before flipping over The wreckage was strewn over an area the size of two football fields. Notley, who sat next to the pilot, died instantly. Archambault, who sat at the rear of the plane, was not injured. He was the first of the survivors to get out. Using survival skills that he had learned as a naval cadet, he cleared a path through the snow and built a fire with two suitcases. He then returned to the upturned plane and helped the injured pilot, Erik Vogel, and housing minister Shaben, who had been knocked unconscious. Archambault also pulled the injured Constable Deschamps out of the wrecked fuselage and carried him over to the fire. "Archambault saved my life," Deschamps said afterwards. "I wouldn't have got out of there by myself."

The survivors huddled shivering in the snow for fourteen hours before a rescue helicopter arrived on the scene. Archambault kept their spirits up, expressing confidence they would be rescued. "All we have to do is make it through to the morning," he said. The only food they had during the ordeal was four chocolate chip cookies brought by the 24-year-old pilot. The plane carried no survival gear because Transport Canada regulations only required such equipment for aircraft flying in what it classified as remote areas.

Pilot Vogel told crash investigators that he had been working for Wapiti for little more than a month, and that he sometimes violated safety regulations because he was afraid of losing his job. He admitted to flying below the minimum altitude required by Transport Canada, and to flying in poor weather without a co-pilot. (That's how Notley ended up in the co-pilot's seat.) Other factors that Vogel felt contributed to the accident were "the pressure to get passengers to their desired destination," his fear of being late, and the threat of dismissal. A Transport Canada official said pilot turnover was so high at Wapiti that the local Canada Employment Centre refused to help the company find replacements. He added that the airline was under "special surveillance" at the time of the crash for repeatedly letting pilots fly in poor weather without co-pilots, and for other safety violations.

Vogel said he knew Transport Canada required planes to be at an altitude of no lower than fifty-six hundred feet to clear obstructions on the flight path into High Prairie. But his bosses had told him that he should fly as low as eight hundred feet in order to see the runway if the visibility was poor higher up, and so he broke the rules. A weather report for that day said there was cloud five hundred feet above the runway and that it was completely overcast at nine hundred. Vogel said he thought he was over the runway when, in fact, he was still eighteen miles from the airport. "I believe that I made an error in navigation," he said. "I believed I was farther ahead than I was."

The Canadian Aviation Safety Board blamed both the pilot and the airline for the crash. It said Vogel was flying too low without knowing exactly where he was, and that Wapiti Aviation failed to ensure that its pilots followed safety rules. The board also criticized Transport Canada's surveillance and audit procedures. It found that although Wapiti was under surveillance because of safety concerns, eight company planes that had been grounded were allowed back into the air three weeks before the crash without verification that the problems had been fixed. The board recommended more follow-ups to ensure that the deficiencies were corrected.

The troubles for Wapiti continued in the following years. In April 1986, Transport Canada suspended the company's operating certificates. The suspension was overturned in a court challenge five weeks later, but the damage was done. In May 1988, the company voluntarily surrendered its operating licence. Owner Dale Wells blamed Transport Canada for damaging Wapiti's reputation, and said he planned to sue the federal government for $4.5 million in lost income. The suit never proceeded.

While Wapiti was being held to account, Archambault was enjoying his day in the sun. Formal recognition for his bravery came in the form of a life-saving certificate from the St. John Ambulance Association of Canada and a letter of commendation from the RCMP. "Your valiant, courageous conduct is a lesson to us all," said the fatality inquiry chairman, Bernard Deschenes. Archambault also heard words of praise from the judge at his trial on charges of mischief and failing to appear in court. "You are to be highly commended for your conduct," said Judge Ken Staples, dismissing the mischief charge and ruling that the five days Archambault spent in custody in Edmonton would serve as sentence enough for his failure to appear in court. "I was surprised at the decision," said Archambault afterwards. "I expected to be locked up for a while."

Archambault had no money in his pockets when he walked out of the courtroom a free man. The sum of $66.35, all the money he had to his name, had been left behind at the Edmonton Remand Centre when he was flown to Grande Prairie. He didn't even have enough cash to use a laundromat and wash the campfire smell out of his clothes. When people read about this in the *Grande Prairie Herald Tribune*, they organized a fund-raising campaign that quickly collected two hundred dollars. Archambault said he planned to remain in Grande Prairie, look for another job, and write a book about his experience entitled, *They Call Me a Hero*.

Archambault never found a publisher for his book. Nor did he find another job in Grand Prairie. He eventually left town and was never heard from again. Pilot Vogel quit his job at Wapiti and returned to his home in White Rock, British Columbia, to collect employment insurance. Housing minister Shaben remained in provincial politics until 1989, after which he became a communications consultant. Constable Deschamps left the RCMP, saying he planned to return to university in British Columbia to complete a master's degree in occupational psychology.

Notley's party did, in fact, eventually make the breakthrough that political observers had predicted shortly before his death. Two years after the plane crash, Alberta voters sent sixteen New Democrats to the provincial legislature. It was as if Notley had finally made the voters realize there could be a viable alternative to the dominant Tories. However, the triumph was short-lived. In succeeding elections, the numbers dwindled and, by the turn of the twenty-first century, the New Democrats were down to just two elected representatives in the legislature.

Canmore Woman Conquers Everest —May 1986

SHARON WOOD CELEBRATED her twenty-ninth birthday on 18 May 1986, standing on a narrow ledge below the summit of Mount Everest, pummelled by strong winds and close to fainting from lack of oxygen. It was an occasion to remember. From a cluster of mountainside campsites below her, colleagues on the Canadian Everest team sang "Happy Birthday" through their two-way radios. She felt happy "and almost completely fulfilled." Two days later she became the first North American woman, and only the sixth woman in history, to conquer the world's highest mountain. That part of the expedition, she said, was an anticlimax. "The climbing to get there had been the exciting part. It was the longest summit climb I had ever been on. At the top we were completely exhausted and the cold was biting through our clothes. It was, like, let's tag the top and get the hell out of here." It was only when she returned to her home in Canmore several weeks later that Wood began to appreciate what she had achieved. "I had gone beyond where I'd gone before, pushed harder, reached deeper than I've ever had to do, and I still had something left. It makes you wonder what our limits really are."

Mount Everest came at the end of a personal journey that began for Wood when she was a child and her father, an avid outdoorsman, took her up her first mountain. Born in Halifax, she moved to the Vancouver suburb of Burnaby with her family when she was seven, and soon discovered that she shared her father's love of skiing and hiking. She didn't like the strip malls and what she saw as the "suburban blight" of Burnaby, so at age sixteen she ran away from home, "just to be in the mountains." She ended up at the Canada Manpower office in Jasper, Alberta, where she applied for a job as a mountain guide. "I had no idea what that was," she conceded afterward. "But I lied about my age and they sent me up to Maligne Lake to work as a guide on a tour boat. I gave talks about geography and history and, on my days off, I would go hiking and rock climbing."

Wood gradually got into high-altitude climbing—defined as scaling heights of eight thousand feet or more—and learned the technical aspects of this male-dominated sport from the likes of Laurie Skreslet, who would later become the first Canadian to climb Everest. Skreslet first met Wood in 1974 when she was seventeen and he was teaching an Outward Bound climbing course in Keremeos, British Columbia. He knew immediately that she was "summit material." He saw her as being "determined, focussed, persevering, and overflowing with potential."

Being a woman in a "man's sport" was never an issue for Wood. She climbed with men because they were the ones climbing at her level. "When you thrust yourself into the world of high-altitude climbing, it doesn't matter whether you are a man or a woman," she said. "The reason we saw only a few North American women on high-altitude climbing teams in the 1970s was that few women climbers had any experience wielding the ice axe."

In 1976, when Wood was nineteen, she became a climbing instructor and guide at what is now Yamnuska, Inc., a mountaineering school based in Canmore, Alberta. Her first break came a year later, when she was part of a team that climbed Mount Logan, Canada's highest peak. But she didn't become serious about her climbing until 1982, when her close friend, John Lauchlan, was killed in an avalanche that swept him off a frozen waterfall. She had been "sitting on the fence about my climbing, and knew I had to either take it seriously or not do it." She followed Lauchlan's advice to "do it right" and became a professional climber.

In 1983, Wood became the first woman certified by the

Association of Canadian Mountain Guides. The same year she went to Alaska and scaled Mount McKinley, the highest mountain in North America. "That really changed my attitude," she said. "I didn't see myself so much as a woman but as a climbing partner. I came back with a lot of confidence." Subsequent climbing expeditions to the Himalayas, Peru, and Argentina convinced Wood that she was "ready for anything." In 1986, she was chosen as a member of the second Canadian team to launch an assault on Everest.

The first Canadian expedition to Everest in 1982, while successful, had been a big, expensive, controversial, and tragedy-filled affair. It had required a $1 million budget, ten tonnes of equipment, and a small army of Sherpa porters to tote the equipment from camp to camp. One man was kicked off the team for alleged drug smuggling, four men died, and six of the fourteen climbers returned home out of respect for the dead. *Mountain* magazine called it "the biggest and most honourable shambles since the retreat from Kabul," the ill-fated 1842 British invasion of Afghanistan that culminated in the withdrawal and virtual destruction of the British troops. But the 1982 expedition did result in a hitherto unknown climber, Skreslet, becoming the first Canadian to place a flag on the summit.

The 1986 expedition, dubbed "Everest Light" because it was one-fifth the size of the 1982 expedition, included Skreslet and four other Canadians—Jim Elzinga, Dwayne Congdon, James Blench, and Dave McNab—who had participated in the first climb. Elzinga was the leader of the twelve-member 1986 team, and he chose Wood to be on the team because of her high-altitude experience. "It didn't matter whether she was male or female," he said. "When we made the first cut, Sharon was number one on our list. All of us had climbed with her and thought she was superbly competent." Wood said she was proud to be part of the team. "Everest is the Olympics in the climber's world."

Plans for the 1986 expedition called for a $300,000 budget, three tonnes of gear and supplies, and no porters or guides. To conserve supplies, the climbers decided they would hold off using oxygen tanks until the final twelve-hour assault on the summit.

Elzinga opted to climb Everest from the north (via Tibet) rather than take the south route (from Nepal) used by the 1982 expedition. While this meant a steeper and more difficult climb, it ultimately proved safer—shielded from the icefalls and avalanches that plagued the first Canadian expedition. After obtaining the necessary permission from the Chinese authorities, and acquiring $100,000 in needed funding from the Continental Bank of Canada, the team began its journey to the top on 19 March 1986. Over the next forty-five days the climbers—working in teams of two—established five camps at strategic points along the route, linking the camps with rope, and stocking them with supplies. It was painstaking, time-consuming, and exhausting work; the kind generally reserved for Sherpas. When it finally came time to try for the summit, only four climbers were still in good enough shape to make it. The rest had fallen victim to chronic nausea, respiratory tract infections, and other ailments caused by prolonged exposure to what Wood called "brutally cold temperatures," thin oxygen, and winds powerful enough to knock the climbers off their feet.

The climbers had taken turns making their way toward the top, and Wood was not initially scheduled to be part of the two-person team going for the summit. However, when Elzinga learned that an American climber, Annie Whitehouse, was poised to make a summit bid during the days following the Canadian attempt, he suggested that one of the Canadian climbers step aside for Wood. She didn't want this but Elzinga was insistent. "For God's sake, don't be so Canadian," he said. "What's the difference between an American and a Canadian? Americans always come first and Canadians second. We can reverse that order on Everest. Here's your chance to make a difference. Go for it." A determined look appeared in Wood's eyes as she exclaimed, "I can outclimb Annie Whitehouse any day."

Wood's partner for the summit bid was Dwayne Congdon, an experienced high-altitude climber who had been part of the 1982 expedition. Helped by two other climbers, all packing up to thirty kilograms of food, oxygen, ropes, and tent gear, they established a sixth camp about two thousand feet from the top, where Wood and Congdon would spend the night before starting their final ascent on the morning of Tuesday, 20 May.

Wood and Congdon started their ascent at 9 AM, communicating by radio to the rest of the team, who were monitoring their progress from a camp ten thousand feet below. "Ya gotta want it," urged Elzinga, his raspy voice crackling through a radio tucked deep inside Wood's jacket. "But don't die for it. No mountain is worth it."

The final climb, up sheer faces of hard-packed ice and snow, was slow going but not too difficult. Along the way, they faced winds of more than 150 kilometres an hour. Wood by then was almost twenty percent lighter than normal because of the high number of calories she burned during the climb. At 9 PM, after twelve hours of climbing, sometimes on all fours, Wood and Congdon walked the last few steps to the 29,025-foot level. "Encumbered in our multiple layers of insulation and our oxygen apparatus, we managed an awkward embrace," said Wood. The sun was setting and they knew they had little time to spend on the top savouring their triumph.

Things began to go wrong as they descended. At twenty-eight thousand feet, Congdon ran out of oxygen. He felt his concentration waning and started moving more slowly, more deliberately. Wood lost patience with him and, because she felt the symptoms of hypothermia setting in, decided to move on by herself. She was so focussed on survival that she didn't realize her radio had stopped working.

With the aid of a miner's headlamp, Wood made it back to camp at 2 AM. Congdon, suffering frostbite in two fingers and severe cold in the rest of his extremities, stumbled in at 3:30 AM. "One of the most pleasant memories I recall was the sound of Dwayne's footsteps outside the tent," said Wood.

But their troubles weren't over yet. At 4 AM, while Wood was preparing to melt snow for drinking water, their pack stove sprang a gas leak and exploded. A flash of flame burned her face and scorched a hole in the roof of the tent. She threw the burning appliance out the front flaps of the tent into the snow. But she threw it too far. It went tumbling off a ledge, down eight thousand feet of mountainside, to a glacier below. The two climbers went without food and water that night.

At dawn, Wood and Congdon got the radio operating again and pushed the button to reestablish contact with the rest of the team. They finished the rest of their descent without incident. Elzinga decided that the others in the crew were too exhausted to provide proper support for a second assault on the summit, so Wood and

Congdon would be the only two members of the expedition to reach the top. The weary team members continued to battle severe storms as they headed back to the base camp on the homeward journey.

Wood moved on to other challenges after Everest. She continued to climb and established a reputation for herself as a motivational speaker, touring North America and talking about her experiences and her approach to risk. "You do not know who you really are until you know what you can fully achieve," she would tell her audiences. "That is what makes living worthwhile."

In 1988, she married Chris Stethem, an avalanche protection expert. They raised two sons and helped create a community school for them and other children in Canmore. In 1997, Wood received the Summit of Excellence Award at the Banff Mountain Film Festival. She was reluctant to accept it at first, because she felt that Everest, once a great symbol of mountaineering achievement, had since become "this trophy for anybody to put on their shelf if they've got the big bucks and the ambition." However, when other winners of the award told her it was not just about climbing Everest, or even about being a woman who had climbed Everest, but about how she had used the Everest climb to tap into other avenues of potential, she felt more comfortable about accepting it. "It's not about me doing anything alone," she said. "It's something that I feel honoured to accept on behalf of a lot of people in my life."

In the Eye of a Tornado
—31 July 1987

Rescue workers sift through debris in the aftermath
of the Edmonton tornado: "It went from a dormant state
to a full-blown tornado and it didn't take one second."

❀

THE FIRST PERSON to identify the cloud as a tornado was a forty-four-year-old Leduc pharmacist named Tom Taylor. It was the Friday afternoon of the 1 August long weekend and Taylor was at home on his acreage, three kilometres northeast of Leduc, getting ready to work the four to midnight shift at NuWay Drugs. The weather in the Edmonton region had been exceptionally hot and muggy during the previous week, with temperatures soaring above thirty degrees Celsius during the day and thunderstorms exploding over the area at night. Taylor fed his Labrador retriever, Snooker, at 2:30 PM and looked up at the darkening sky. "Looks like the storm could be blowing in early today," he thought. He went inside, fixed himself a sandwich for supper, and doffed his clothes to take a bath. As he lowered himself into the tub, he could hear rain and hailstones hitting the metal chimney, and thunder that got louder with every clap. He quickly jumped out of the tub, thinking it might not be the safest place to be in a thunderstorm.

The rain stopped as suddenly as it had started. From his second-floor window Taylor could see a large cloud gathering to the south over Leduc and a smaller cloud, resembling a wasp's nest, hanging below it. The rope-shaped tail of the nest corkscrewed toward the ground, touched down briefly, sucked up debris, and exploded. "It was incredible," Taylor told a friend afterwards. "It went from a dormant state to a full-blown tornado and it didn't take one second. It was like turning on a switch."

At five minutes to three, Taylor called Environment Canada's weather office at the Edmonton International Airport. He reached meteorologist Garry Atchison, head of the office's "severe weather" team. "I've just seen a funnel," said Taylor, "and it touched the ground." Atchison had been tracking the storm on radar as it travelled north from Red Deer and had issued periodic weather advisories

162

about hail, lightning, and damaging winds. Now he knew he had been watching something more serious. "I better get a tornado warning out," he said. He dispatched the message to local radio and television stations at 3:07 PM. By then the tornado had embarked along a forty-kilometre path of destruction that would result in twenty-seven deaths, hundreds of injuries, more than one thousand homeless, and $330 million in property damage.

Taylor stood on his garage roof and watched the tornado for another twenty minutes as it swung northward toward Beaumont, a farming community just south of Edmonton. The storm continued on toward the southeast Edmonton subdivision of Mill Woods, beyond which Taylor could see the flare stacks of Refinery Row and the skyscrapers of Edmonton's downtown. He snapped a few photographs and then drove into Leduc to start his shift. The pharmacy cashier didn't believe him when he told her he had just seen a tornado.

The tornado sucked up cattle and swept them to their deaths as it passed through Beaumont. In Mill Woods, it ripped roofs off houses and shredded fences. It unleashed its full force when it reached the industrial district located between Edmonton and the suburban municipality of Sherwood Park, eight kilometres to the east. It sucked cars and tractor-trailers into the air, picked up oil storage tanks and bounced them like beach balls, reduced buildings to kindling, and killed several people.

The biggest single loss of life—fourteen deaths—occurred when the tornado hit the Evergreen Mobile Home Park, a 720-residence development surrounded by farmers' fields and nurseries in the city's northeastern corner. The park's seventeen hundred inhabitants had no basements in which to hide and not enough warning to get out of the storm's path.

Evergreen resident Marin Athanasopoulos, a dark-haired, thirty-year-old mother of four, was at home with her children, writing a letter to her mother-in-law in Ontario, when the tornado hit. Her two oldest boys, eleven-year-old Robert and five-year-old George were playing in the front yard while two-year-old Joseph and baby Kosta, ten months old, were in the house sleeping. At 3:40 PM the power in the park went off. "Here we go again, the power is always going off in this place," Marin said to herself. "Now we can't eat the supper in the oven, so we'll just have to have a picnic. We'll spread a blanket on the living room floor and have some fun." She looked out the living-room window and saw big dark clouds racing across the sky. "Check this out," she said to Robert as he and George came in from the yard. "I've never seen clouds moving that fast before."

Down the street, the wind plucked a roof from a house and tossed it into the air. Marin watched it fly and then ran outside to put away the children's toys. The wind flung her against the gate and carried away the toys. She shut the door of the garden shed just as its roof blew off. She had asked her husband to fix the roof because she knew it was coming loose, and clearly he hadn't done it properly. She thought of the choice words she would use to reprimand him when he got home from work. He worked as a cook at Capital Pizza and was due home at 6:30 PM.

Kosta was awake and crying in his crib as she went back into the house. She lifted him up, carried him into the living room, and sat with him watching the storm. The eaves trough extended four feet out from the roof, and she could see it shaking and starting to bend. "Oh, no," she said. "We should have cut that thing off. It's going to hit our car." The car, normally driven by her husband, had recently received a new paint job. He had taken her old car to work so that the newly painted car wouldn't get dented or scratched. She yelled at Robert to grab her car keys from the kitchen. She could hear windows starting to break throughout the house. The sound of the storm was so loud that she felt like she was standing under the engine of a jet airplane. She cradled the baby in her arms and ran down the hallway toward the wing that had been added to their trailer home. Two-year-old Joseph was in the wing, lying in a bunk bed. While she ran she felt the house bouncing up and down like popcorn in a machine. Behind her, the living room furniture was being sucked out one window while someone else's furniture was coming in through another. Wooden two by fours were coming through the walls. The park outside was shrouded in darkness.

Robert and George ran behind her. Robert was shouting, "Here's the keys. Here's the keys." Marin stopped, turned, took the car keys from Robert, put them on top of the freezer, and handed the baby to Robert. "You stay there while I check on Joseph," she said. She carried on alone into the back wing and snatched up the two-year-old from his bed. As they came out through the doorway the wing collapsed behind them. Marin would learn later that the trailer home next door had landed on top of the wing. At that point her home briefly stopped bouncing. "What is it? What is it?" asked Robert. Marin decided she knew what it was because she had seen this scene in *The Wizard of Oz.* "It's a tornado," she said quietly.

She remembered what her uncle in Michigan had said to her about staying safe in a tornado: "You go to the basement or you stand in a doorway." She didn't have a basement, so she stood in her bedroom doorway hugging her children close. Through the window they could see a trailer home shooting up into the air and blowing apart. Their house had started bouncing again. Marin started praying. "Please God, don't leave some of my babies to wake up in this mess and find the rest of us dead," she said. "Don't do that to my babies. If this is the end, make it the end for all of us."

The house finally stopped bouncing and the roaring outside stopped. It had seemed like an eternity but it had taken just ten minutes for the tornado to churn through the park. A deathly silence blanketed the park. The children started to cry. Marin checked each one of them for possible injuries and then started clawing through the rubble. "My neighbours will be on the other side digging, because I've seen this on TV," she thought. "You dig, they dig, and then you meet in the middle."

When she got through the rubble, there were no neighbours to meet her on the other side. All she could see was more rubble and what looked like human figures growing out of the piles of garbage. "I don't know what's going on," she thought. "Maybe we've been bombed.... But why would they bomb us? It doesn't make sense; why would they bomb Evergreen?" Then she remembered that that the park had been hit by a tornado.

Her uncle had told her that tornadoes could sometimes come in sequence. "That twister can come back," she thought, momentarily panic-stricken. "I've got to get my kids out of here." But they were in summer clothes with bare feet. She couldn't have them walking through the garbage and the rubble like that. She took the children back through the ruins of her house to look for coats and shoes. She could feel a scream emanating from deep inside her, but she held it in check because she didn't want the children to know she was afraid. "I can't be upset," she thought. "I have to act normal." She dressed the children in coats and shoes and then went back outside into the pouring rain.

A mountain of twisted metal, drywall, paper, glass, and wooden debris blocked the approach to the strip mall, near the entrance to the park. As Marin came close to it she realized it was all that remained of the home where her babysitter, Edith, had lived. Did Edith make it out safely? That's when Marin lost control. She uttered a long and anguished scream. She held son Joseph in her left arm and started clawing through the rubble with her right hand. "I've got to find my babysitter," she shrieked. A man gently pushed her away from the debris. "You can't help," he said. "You need to look after your children." Marin would learn later that Edith was safe.

She entered the Evergreen Supermarket, and looked for a roll of paper towel to wipe the rain from her eyeglasses. There was nobody behind the counter. "He won't mind if I take some towel," she thought. "I'll pay him later." She sat the two youngest children on the counter and went to fetch the towel. But, the older children screamed at her to come back. They pointed to a man lying on the floor with a two by four impaling his chest. Marin grabbed the children and ran from the store. They made their way to the park entrance.

When they arrived at the park entrance, Marin spotted an Edmonton police constable sitting in a cruiser. She walked up to him and said, "My name is Marin Athanasopoulos, and these are my four children, Robert, George, Joseph, and Kosta. We lived in number thirty-four. Where do we register?"

The officer looked perplexed. "Register?" he said.

"Yes, we're survivors in a disaster," said Marin, repeating her name and the names of her children. "We need to register that we're safe. My husband will be looking for us."

She asked the policeman if the tornado had hit downtown

Edmonton. "No," he replied. "The city's fine."

"Then my husband will be coming for us," said Marin. "We'll be on the bus. Would you please tell him that that's where we are?" She steered the children toward the waiting Edmonton Transit bus. She sat with the children at the back of the bus, where she thought they would be safe if the tornado came back.

Through the window of the bus she saw a man in a yellow raincoat carrying a bleeding and bruised baby. Marin recognized the week-old infant as the daughter of a sixteen-year-old girl who had done some babysitting for her. Marin ran to the front door of the bus.

"You should give me that baby, I know her mother," she said to the man. The baby was soaked from the rain, and clad only in a diaper and T-shirt.

"You'll have to keep her nasal passages clear," he said. "I had to clear her passages twice already."

The baby gurgled, rolled back her eyes, and stopped breathing just as Marin took her aboard the bus. Panic-stricken and unsure about how to clear the baby's passages, Marin poked a finger down her throat. The baby coughed, vomited, and started breathing again. Relieved but still concerned that the baby might die, Marin carried her away from the bus and handed her to the policeman, a constable named Bill Clark.

"What's her name?" asked Clark.

"I can't remember," replied Marin.

"That's all right," said Clark. He took a yellow survival blanket from his trunk and wrapped the baby in it. The baby was struggling to breathe and seemed to be in pain.

Clark radioed for an ambulance. "We don't have any," said the dispatcher. "They're all tied up." Clark decided to perform ambulance duty himself. He put the baby in his lap and turned the key in the ignition. He told Marin he would take the baby to the Royal Alexandra Hospital.

Clark drove toward the hospital at top speed, weaving through stalled traffic like a rally driver and bouncing over grass medians. The trip seemed to take forever. Every road in northeast Edmonton was littered with downed trees and power lines. Every underpass was flooded. Clark held the steering wheel with one hand

and gently pulled on the baby's fingers and toes with the other until the cruiser reached the hospital. If the baby winced, he knew she was still alive. The baby survived. Fourteen at Evergreen did not.

The bus took Marin and her children and the other tornado refugees to nearby Alberta Hospital, a psychiatric facility. Marin had left the trailer park without her purse so she asked a nurse to give her a quarter to phone her husband. It was now dinnertime and the restaurant was busy. A waitress answered the phone and then sent word back to the kitchen that Marin's husband, Denis, should take the call. He was not happy to be pulled away from the kitchen during the busiest period of his working day and, like many Edmontonians, did not yet know that a tornado had struck the city. Marin assured him that she and the children were safe, asked him to phone her parents, and said she would meet him at the restaurant when the hospital staff cleared them for release.

Denis didn't wait for Marin and the children to get there. When he finished his shift he jumped in his car and arrived at the hospital just as someone was shouting that another tornado was about to hit. Scared and screaming, the survivors and hospital staff ran downstairs into the tunnels that connected different parts of the hospital. They cowered there for half an hour until a false alarm was declared.

When Marin was finally released from the hospital she told Denis that she needed to go back to Evergreen to fetch her purse and pick up diapers and formula for the baby. They had to go via a back road because police and emergency vehicles blocked the front entrance. Marin stared sadly at her broken home. It was still standing, with someone else's trailer piled on top of what had been the children's bedroom. Worried about looters, she stuffed as many valuables as he could into a sleeping bag, along with the diapers, clothing, and bottles.

They stayed the night at a friend's house and returned to Evergreen the following day to retrieve some more of their belongings. A woman from Alberta Victim Services accompanied them to the home, and told Marin what items she should look for: "Do you know where your marriage licence is? Your birth certificate? Jewelry?" Marin didn't know where any of those things were. But in the bathroom cupboard she knew she had some toilet paper that she had bought on sale for twenty cents a roll. "If I don't get my toilet paper, I didn't get a good sale," said Marin. "And if I don't get the margarine from my freezer, that won't have been a good sale either." The woman assured her that the toilet paper and the margarine would be put to good use. "You should look for the things that have a greater meaning for you; the things that will help you put your life back together."

Marin and her family remained homeless for the next two months. The Red Cross put them up in a hotel for a couple of weeks, and their insurance paid for an apartment rental while they waited to move back to Evergreen. A friend told her she should use the insurance money and provincial government compensation to buy a house in Edmonton, but Marin was determined to move back.

"I live in Evergreen for a reason," she said. "It's a beautiful, quiet, country-living, safe neighbourhood to raise my children. That's why I moved there and no windstorm is going to scare me away. I'm going right back there. I'm not going to be scared away and made to live in the city. I don't like the city. I like where I live." She told her children that God had protected them from the tornado because they had a Palm Sunday wreath on their front door and a statue of the Last Supper in the living room.

It would be fifteen years before the nightmares would go away, fifteen years before Marin could listen to thunder without panicking, fifteen years before she could resist the urge to flee whenever a storm approached Evergreen. But for now she had a role to play, advocating for tornado victims without insurance, lobbying government officials, speaking to the media, attending memorial services, holding hands, comforting those who lost loved ones, participating in support group sessions, and telling people over and over again that there is a rainbow at the end of every storm.

It was the least she could do.

The Principal Group Collapse: The Man Who Knew—August 1987

A Principal Trust investor learns that the company
has declared bankruptcy: "Agreements continually
violated and ignored."

WHEN THE PRINCIPAL Group financial empire went bankrupt in 1987 more than sixty-seven thousand Canadians were shocked to discover that their life savings, amounting to $457 million, were in jeopardy. One man, however, could have said, "I told you so." He was Jim Darwish, a former Alberta government regulator who had spent twenty-five years warning his political bosses about the Principal conglomerate's shady business practices.

The Principal Group began life in 1954 as an Edmonton-based investment company, First Investors Corporation, which sold budget installment savings plans to people of modest means. A typical plan, similar to an insurance policy with a cash surrender value, would commit a person to save a few dollars a month over a specified number of years. At the end of that time the plan holder would receive the total saved plus interest. The plan holder had no direct stake in any of the company's investments, so each plan was in effect an IOU payable by the company at maturity.

The company sold its savings plans—which it called "investment contracts"—to clients in Alberta and Saskatchewan, and the business grew rapidly. By 1958 the company was managing contracts valued at more than two million dollars. Forty five percent of the company's shares were controlled by president Donald Cormie, a Harvard-educated Edmonton lawyer who had acquired his first business experience as a twenty-one-year-old university student working as secretary-treasurer for his father's mill company, North West Mill and Feed. After graduating from Harvard in 1946, at age twenty-four, Cormie articled with an Edmonton law firm and worked there for seven years.

In 1954, Cormie established his own practice, in partnership with a lawyer named Jack Kennedy, and began to specialize in real estate, commercial, and securities law. When he founded First

Investors, his partners included Kennedy, former World Bank executive Ralph Forster, realtor Stan Melton, and chartered accountant Cliff Willetts.

In the fall of 1959, First Investors expanded into the United States. It couldn't use the name First Investors because there was already a company by that name operating in the United States, so it took the name Principal for its American operations. It started with an office in Seattle and then opened offices in other parts of Washington, and in Oregon and Colorado. At this time, the company also opened offices in Nova Scotia, New Brunswick, and Newfoundland.

Toward the end of 1959, Cormie and his three partners sold their First Investors' shares to a holding company they owned called Collective Securities. It was a deal that regulator Darwish would later call a "well-watered" stock transaction. The partners sold their shares at six times the original cost and thus grossly inflated the book value of Collective Securities.

At around the same time, in late 1959, Darwish began scrutinizing the operations of Cormie's companies. Darwish was a thirty-year-old chartered accountant who had joined the Alberta government in 1949 as a messenger carrying documents back and forth between officials in the Department of Public Welfare. He was bright and energetic and showed such an aptitude for figures that his boss suggested he might use this talent to do some bookkeeping work for the department. He studied accounting at night, articled with the Provincial Auditor for five years, and became a chartered accountant in 1956 at age twenty-seven. He spent two years as an income tax officer with the federal government and then joined the Alberta Securities Commission as an auditor.

The Securities Commission was then the provincial authority responsible for regulating Alberta companies selling investment contracts. Darwish worked there for about a dozen years and was said to have the ideal temperament for a government regulator because, in the words of former deputy minister Jack Lyndon, he was "an honest, very hardworking son-of-a-bitch." Lyndon said his term of endearment for Darwish was "my favourite nitpicking accountant. He and I had a delightful relationship of dynamic tension. We didn't always agree on things, but I did give him his head."

Darwish was handed the First Investors' file as part of his initial auditing responsibilities for the Securities Commission, and right away he noticed that something seemed to be wrong. Under the province's Investment Contracts Act the company was supposed to maintain up to half a million dollars in cash or other assets in its bank account to cover its liability to contract holders. Yet Darwish noticed that increases in First Investors' share capital had been achieved through a series of paper transactions in which no money actually changed hands. Author Wendy Smith illustrated the strategy as follows in her book, *Pay Yourself First: Donald Cormie and the Collapse of the Principal Group of Companies*:

> If I buy a mongrel puppy for a dollar and sell it to you in exchange for an IOU of $1,000, and you sell the puppy to your uncle for an IOU of $1,000, and he sells the puppy back to me for an IOU of $1,000—is there $1,000 anywhere? Certainly not. There's just a mongrel puppy, a dollar bill, and a lot of damp paper.

Aside from these inflated increases in share capital, Darwish noticed that company officers paid themselves high salaries and were withdrawing huge amounts of company money to pay off personal bank loans. In a 1961 memo to his supervisors, Darwish complained about exorbitant management fees paid to companies owned or controlled by Cormie, and warned that more cash or other assets would have to be put into First Investors to meet the financial requirements of the Investment Contracts Act. Cormie didn't like such regulatory interference in his affairs but he did undertake to comply with the requirements of the Act. It was an empty pledge. Alberta Ombudsman Aleck Trawick would report later that the company "followed a pattern of operating to the very outside limits of the legislation and of challenging the regulators on every matter raised."

The creation of Collective Securities was Cormie's first step in the development of an increasingly elaborate corporate structure. The most significant layer in the system was created in 1966 when

Principal Group Ltd. (with Cormie as president) was inserted as a holding and management company between Collective and its subsidiaries. Principal Group was designed as a vehicle that would provide complete one-stop personal financial services to customers. It billed itself as "The Department Store of Finance." Its subsidiaries included, along with First Investors and Associated Investors of Canada (a 1962 Collective acquisition), two Canadian mutual fund companies and Principal Savings and Trust Ltd. The savings and trust subsidiary soon became the flagship company in the burgeoning Principal conglomerate and would later become synonymous with one of the biggest collapses in Canadian financial history.

As the company grew, so did the headaches for Darwish and his fellow regulators. In 1966, Darwish's boss, Securities Commission Chairman Harry Rose, wrote a memo to Alberta's Deputy Attorney General, John Hart, saying that Darwish had uncovered evidence of "manipulative practices designed to create a false picture of the status" of First Investors and Associated Investors. Millions of dollars in dividends were being paid to shareholders out of paper profits, and "exorbitant" management fees were being paid to related companies in which Cormie had a direct or indirect interest. Rose expressed frustration over Cormie's unwillingness to acknowledge "what I consider totally improper conduct in operating these two companies." However, Hart never took any action on Rose's memo. He said there was obviously a "serious personality conflict" between Cormie and the government regulators. A few years later, Hart retired from government service and went to work for Cormie as general counsel.

The Securities Commission did achieve a victory of sorts when it threatened to suspend the operating licences of First Investors and Associated Investors, and forced Cormie's associates to return three hundred thousand dollars in management fees taken from one of the companies. The Commission also extracted a promise from Cormie that the questionable intercorporate transactions would cease. But the victory was short-lived. The companies were soon living beyond their means again, borrowing from Peter to pay Paul. They borrowed to pay off maturing investment contracts while simultaneously loaning money and paying dividends and management fees to related companies.

Darwish left the Securities Commission in 1972 and moved to the Department of Consumer and Corporate Affairs where he was appointed superintendent of insurance and real estate. Responsibility for the Investment Contracts Act was transferred to Darwish's office a year later, so once again he found himself dealing with the Cormie companies. Between 1973 and 1975, Darwish and his fellow regulators sent a series of reports to provincial cabinet ministers expressing concern about the financial standing of First Investors and Associated Investors. In 1974, Darwish suggested that every Principal Group company be audited "so that the government will have the total picture." In 1975, he urged that the Attorney General be called in to investigate whether "there has been a breach of trust or other Criminal Code violations." A report by an external auditor had led Darwish to conclude that the assets of the companies were over-valued by millions of dollars and that the companies were seriously deficient in terms of being able to meet certificate liabilities at maturity. The Attorney General never did become involved, but the regulators' reports did result in strict new guidelines being established for the Principal companies and a timetable being set for compliance.

Darwish continued to worry that investors' money might be at risk. He had reached what he thought was a "gentleman's agreement" with Principal officials that the companies would operate with a debt-to-equity ratio of twenty-five to one (meaning they could borrow up to twenty-five dollars for every dollar invested). However, the agreement was—as Alberta Ombudsman Aleck Trawick noted later—"continually violated and ignored." In 1984, one of Darwish's auditors, Allan Hutchison, reported that the two Principal Group units were "virtually insolvent" and had a "staggering" debt-to-equity ratio of 560 to one. The companies held a total of $18.8 million in foreclosed mortgages following the collapse of the Alberta real estate market in the early 1980s. In all, seventy-one percent of their entire mortgage portfolio was in arrears and forty-two percent was in foreclosure.

Hutchison estimated that if First Investors were liquidated, its debts would exceed its assets by more than $73 million. He recommended appraisals on all mortgages that were six months or more in arrears, and urged that the companies be made to comply with the

175

Investment Contracts Act's capital requirements. Darwish, who was now an assistant deputy minister, sought a meeting with Connie Osterman, the minister of Consumer and Corporate Affairs, to explain the urgency of the situation. When she didn't reply, he sent her a memorandum listing conditions with which the companies should immediately comply or have their licences pulled. Among them was a demand that the companies reverse a transaction in which First Investors and Associated Investors paid $23 million to Principal Savings and Trust for nineteen mortgages and four properties of dubious value.

Osterman reacted furiously. In a telephone conversation on 30 April 1984, she told Darwish that she didn't want any more advice from him. "If you keep making these recommendations, you're going to have to make a career decision," she said. "You're on the outside looking in. I have had discussions with company officials, and you don't have a clue about the other side of this." This was an apparent reference to a luncheon meeting Osterman had a couple of months previously with Cormie and some of his vice-presidents.

Principal's executives had always enjoyed a friendly relationship with Alberta politicians. Over the years, Cormie and his associates had often sought relief from what they perceived as unreasonable demands from hostile public servants, and they had repeatedly warned that the province's entire financial services industry would be endangered if the Principal companies were hurt. This warning struck a sympathetic chord with the politicians because Alberta had a long history of favouring homegrown savings companies and credit unions over eastern financial institutions. Rather than rewrite and strengthen what the regulators regarded as an inadequate Investment Contracts Act, the politicians left their civil servants to make "gentlemen's agreements" that invariably turned out to be shams.

Darwish interpreted Osterman's telephone remarks as a threat to get rid of him. Six months later he took early retirement at age fifty-five. There was no retirement party to honour his thirty-five years of government service. Only his wife and a few of his colleagues knew that he had left involuntarily.

The Principal companies limped along for another two years after Darwish's departure. Regulators continued to ask for an independent investigator to look at the companies but were told that Osterman would not authorize one "because it would cause a run on the companies." The companies lost $13.6 million in the first nine months of 1985. In June 1986, responsibility for the Investment Contracts Act shifted from Consumer and Corporate Affairs to Alberta Treasury. In November, an accountant was finally hired to determine whether the companies could survive.

The accountant reported that the companies would need at least $150 million to stay afloat. Cormie tried to negotiate government aid but to no avail. On 30 June 1987, Treasurer Dick Johnston cancelled the operating licences of First Investors and Associated Investors. Six weeks later Principal Group declared bankruptcy.

Calgary lawyer Bill Code was appointed by the courts to conduct one inquiry, and the provincial ombudsman, Aleck Trawick, did a separate investigation. Darwish was a key witness. He struggled to hold back tears when he testified about his April 1984 phone conversation with Osterman. "She was agitated. As a matter of fact she was yelling at me," said Darwish. "I feel that I was fired or forced out." Osterman acknowledged that her reaction to Darwish's memo was "reasonably negative" because she felt he was interfering as assistant deputy minister in areas that were no longer his concern.

The Code investigation found "evidence tending to prove" that Cormie and his partners had defrauded investors with misleading sales pitches, and had evaded taxes and manipulated stock markets. It also accused Osterman of being "neglectful and misguided" when she refused to act on the recommendations of her subordinates. Trawick praised Darwish and his colleagues for reporting "thoroughly and tenaciously" in the face of a "clear failure" by their superiors to "heed or in some instances to understand" their warnings.

Darwish was jubilant. "It was one of the best things that ever happened to me," he said. "I was able to stick by what I thought was right and, in the end, I was vindicated. It wasn't that I felt that I had to be vindicated but it's nice to have a couple of third parties agree with what you did," he said.

Premier Don Getty dismissed Osterman from his cabinet one week after the Code report came out in July 1989. At the same time he announced a partial compensation to Alberta investors of fifteen to eighteen cents on every dollar invested. Cormie pleaded guilty under the Investors Act to misleading investors and was fined half a million dollars. The Tax Court of Canada ordered him to pay $4 million in back taxes on a $7.2 million loan he took from Principal just before it collapsed. A Court of Queen's Bench judge ruled that he made improper payouts totalling half a million dollars to creditors who were family members or company employees, and ordered that the creditors give back the money.

It took fourteen years before the investors received their final payments. Most of them were elderly people who had entrusted their retirement savings to Principal. Seventy-five percent of them lived in Alberta, with the rest in British Columbia, Saskatchewan, and the Maritimes. At the end of the day, the Albertans obtained about ninety cents for every dollar invested, with no compensation for any interest that might have accumulated. Investors in other provinces received less because their provincial governments set aside a smaller amount of money to reimburse them.

Darwish sued the province for $7,678 in back holiday pay and won. The severance package he negotiated with the Alberta government included about a year's salary and full government pension, allowing him to ease comfortably into retirement. He then took on a new role, challenging the Alberta government on environmental issues. He became a volunteer with Edmonton Friends of the North Environmental Society, fighting pulp mills, pollution, hazardous waste disposal, and the industrialization of agriculture. In 1993, the Rotary Club of Edmonton chose him as the recipient of its first Integrity Award.

The Eagle of the Winter Olympics—February 1988

꙳

AN AUSTRALIAN JOURNALIST suggested that the name of the sport should be changed to "ski dropping." A novice British ski jumper named Michael ("Eddie the Eagle") Edwards had arrived in Calgary for the Winter Olympics and astonished onlookers with a free-fall technique that might have been patented by Chuckles the Clown. Media commentators wondered how British Olympic Association officials could have selected such a bumbling klutz to wear their country's colours in the Games. "He should change his nickname to Eddie the Emu because it doesn't fly either," said the Australian journalist.

It turned out that Edwards was indeed a legitimate member of the British Olympic squad although the officials were almost embarrassed to say so. He had qualified for the event by recording a seventy-one-metre jump—short by Olympic standards but nonetheless the minimum required—while competing in Austria during the summer of 1987. Because no other British ski jumper applied, Edwards automatically made the Olympic team for 1988.

Before Edwards came on the scene, the talk leading up the 1988 Games was all about medal prospects. Would the great East German figure-skating star Katarina Witt defeat her American archrival, Debi Thomas? Would top-rated Canadian skater Brian Orser beat the American challenger, Brian Boitano? And would Italy's Alberto Tomba, the playboy they called La Bomba, win a gold medal in the alpine skiing events?

As it turned out, Witt did win gold in the women's figure-skating singles (surpassing the upstart Canadian, Elizabeth Manley, who unexpectedly edged out Thomas for the silver); Orser suffered a heartbreaking loss to Boitano in the men's singles; and Tomba captured not one but two golds in the men's slalom events. But while much of the media talk after the Games was about those who made it or should have made it onto the winners' podium, the talk among the fans was about the crazy ski-jumping Englishman who went from being a minor curiosity to an improbable folk hero. "The last shall be first—at least in the hearts of the eighty-thousand people who crowded the Canada Olympic Park jumping bowl," reported a Calgary tabloid the day after Edwards came last of fifty-eight competitors in the seventy-metre event. (The Englishman jumped fifty-five metres while the gold-medal winner, Finland's Matti Nykanen, jumped 89.5 metres.) The fans liked Edwards for what he was: a working-class Everyman from Cheltenham, Gloucestershire, who flew in the face of fear and insecurity and made his way to the Olympics through a combination of pluck, determination, and a refusal to be denied a chance to compete.

Edwards had been ski jumping for less than three years when he qualified for the British Olympic team. He had taken up the sport in the fall of 1985 as an inexpensive alternative to downhill skiing, which he decided he could ill afford. The son of a Cheltenham plasterer, he first tried downhill skiing at age fourteen when he went on a school trip to the Italian Alps, and from that point onward he skied at every opportunity, on a plastic-covered slope near his home. A part-time job at this artificial ski hill and a twice-daily paper route gave him the money he needed to finance his hobby.

When he turned eighteen, Edwards landed a winter job at an Italian ski resort, in a shop that rented out skis, boots, and poles to vacationing British school children. This position allowed him to develop his skiing skills on snow rather than on plastic, and he took full advantage of the opportunity. He spent three winters in Italy, combining ski training with his work at the rental shop, and spent his summers in England working on building sites with his father. He won a few downhill races in Britain, skiing on plastic slopes, and then aimed his sights at the Winter Olympics. His parents agreed to support him financially while he concentrated full-time on realizing his ambition to become an Olympic challenger.

After four years of racing in Britain and Europe, Edwards moved to Lake Placid, New York. He had found it tough competing in Europe and figured he would have a better chance of earning World Cup qualifying points in the United States, where he considered the standards to be lower. However, lift tickets and downhill equipment turned out to be more expensive in New York than in Europe, and Edwards soon realized that his parents would go bankrupt if they had to keep supporting him there. That's when he switched from racing to ski jumping. Coached by a former American Olympian named John Viscome, Edwards trained free of charge for a few months at Lake Placid and then moved back to Europe, where it was cheaper to live.

Ski jumping didn't come easily to him. In fact, Edwards endeared himself to would-be jumpers everywhere when he told a British television interviewer that he shook with fear whenever he stood at the top of a ninety-metre tower (a height equivalent, he said, to that of St. Paul's Cathedral in London) and looked at the tiny dots of people far below. "My bottom wrinkles up like a prune as every muscle in my body tightens." But Edwards was determined to overcome his fear and make his mark in a sport where he felt there was a chance he might establish himself as a British champion. While ski-jumping competitions were almost never seen in Britain—the sport there, according to one commentator, was "almost as popular as curling in Egypt"—the records revealed that there was one long-forgotten British ski-jumping champion on the books: an athlete named Guy Dixon who had jumped sixty-one metres at a competition in Switzerland in 1936.

By the time Edwards arrived in Calgary in 1988, he had eclipsed Dixon's fifty-two-year-old British record and had begun to take on the status of a cult figure. He had competed in several World Cup events in Europe and—contrary to later media reports that he came last in every one—had actually managed to do better in these competitions than some of the Spanish, Dutch, Hungarian, and Bulgarian jumpers. Readers of London's newspapers couldn't get enough of the story of this eccentric British ski jumper who bummed around Europe to practice his skills, and BBC Television discovered that Edwards was also a popular draw on the supper-hour news.

Contributing to the appeal of the Edwards story was his goofy snaggletoothed appearance, his reckless-abandonment technique, and his cheerful admission that he risked breaking his neck every time he jumped. "But I've got to do it for the crowds and for ski jumping." He wore pink-framed eyeglasses as big as ski goggles, both on the ski-jump runway and off, and said they often fogged up just as he was about leap into the great unknown. "But they sometimes clear enough for me to see where I'll land, and on which part of my body." En route to the Olympics he had broken arms, hands, fingers, feet, and jaw, and almost ended his career with a fall in which he fractured bones in his back and neck. "I'm still learning to cope with the fear that the next jump could be my last," he said.

The stories of the madcap Englishman's penchant for attracting disaster abounded after he arrived in Calgary. His suitcase burst open on the airport carousel and the television cameras rolled unsympathetically as he scrambled to retrieve his clothing. The other members of the British Olympic team had to go looking for him when he lost his way in the Olympic Village. He missed two of three scheduled practice rounds because his ski bindings arrived in a state of disrepair. And he was refused admission to his first-ever press conference, at the Olympic Saddledome, because he didn't have proper accreditation. "You couldn't possibly be an athlete," insisted the security guard while British Olympic officials protested that the small bewildered myopic individual with the big pink glasses was indeed the ski jumper, "Eddie the Eagle" Edwards.

The reporters' questions yielded some choice answers when Edwards finally gained admittance to his own press conference. In the absence of sponsorship how did he finance his ski-jumping activities? "By plastering walls, washing dishes, babysitting, and getting money from me mum and dad." Where did he acquire his equipment? "It was all donated. The Italians fixed me up with a helmet, the West Germans gave me a ski suit, and the Austrians gave me the skis. You could call me a true international competitor." What was his training diet? "The usual English delicacies: beans on toast, egg on toast, bread and jam." Was it true that he once broke his jaw during a ski jump, and then tied it up with a borrowed pillowcase? "Yes, I couldn't find a proper bandage." And how about the rumour that he stayed at a psychiatric hospital while training in Finland because it cost him less than $2 a night? "Yes, I had to lock the door to keep out the patients."

Not everyone was amused. The International Ski Federation threatened to ban him—for his own safety, it said—from the ninety-metre competition. Edwards competed anyhow, and, predictably, came in last, just as he had in the seventy-metre event. He also tried competing in the team-jumping event, but this time the officials put their feet down and refused him entry. One jumper does not constitute a team, they said.

The East German newspaper, *Junge Welt*, wasn't amused either. While the Canadian, English and American newspapers hailed Edwards as the embodiment of the Olympic ideal—an athlete who was in it for the challenge, not for the medals—*Junge Welt* denounced him as a "clown" whose "antics" could debase the Games: "What would become of the Games if the Eddie Edwardses of the world took their place in every discipline and so discredited the achievements of all those who far outstripped them in ability?" A London newspaper, *The Star*, responded that Edwards should be acclaimed as a "true grit Brit who has put a warm smile on the Winter Olympics in Calgary."

Along with the press attention came what Edwards viewed as exploitation. The most notable instance occurred when he naively accepted an invitation to what he thought would be a quiet dinner at a Calgary hotel, and unexpectedly found himself on stage with the "Eaglelettes" dancers (a group of models used by the tabloid *Calgary Sun* for self-promotion purposes and known, just a few weeks earlier, as the "Red, White and Hots"). "That annoyed me and, probably more than anything else, made me aware of how difficult life can be in the spotlight," said Edwards. He hired a London agent, Simon Platz, and started to do some exploiting of his own. He sold his life story to a London newspaper, the *Daily Mail*, for a reported US $65,000, and landed a book contract with the Weidenfeld and Nicolson publishing house to write his autobiography.

The president of the International Olympic Committee, Juan Antonio Samaranch, was said to be privately critical of Edwards for appearing to mock the Games with his inept performance. But Samaranch seemed to embrace the British jumper during his speech at the closing ceremonies. "At Calgary people set new goals, created new world records, and some even flew like an eagle," he said to raucous applause.

A tumultuous homecoming awaited Edwards after he left Calgary. Nobody in the crowd waiting to greet him at Heathrow airport seemed to notice that members of the rock band U2 were arriving at the same time. A big parade through the streets of Cheltenham was followed by an appearance on the top-rated BBC talk show *Wogan* (Edwards had earlier been a guest on the American *Tonight Show Starring Johnny Carson)* and a trip to a recording studio to cut a single entitled "Fly, Eddie, Fly." That song, like his jumping career, failed to take off but a second recording, "Mun Niemi En Eetu" ("My name is Eddie"), actually reached the number-two spot on the Finland hit parade in 1991.

The media coverage continued for months and years after Edwards returned to England. In one story, he announced that he was considering an offer of free plastic surgery to reduce his jutting chin and cheekbones, and was hoping to work in Hollywood as "Robert Redford's stunt man." In another story, he said he would pose nude for the magazine *Playgirl* if he were paid $1 million. He continued to compete in World Cup events and said he planned to be a serious contender at the 1992 Winter Olympics in Albertville, France.

Edwards never made it to the Albertville Olympics. The International Ski Federation instituted what has become informally known as the "Eddie the Eagle rule," requiring Olympic hopefuls to finish among the top fifty percent of jumpers in an international competition, and this effectively eliminated Edwards from future Games. But he did help create a new market for the sport in Britain. Several young British athletes took up the sport during the 1990s, artificial ski-jumping facilities were built in England and Scotland, and Britain's second Olympic jumper (a Canadian of English-born parentage) competed in the 2002 Winter Games in Salt Lake City. Edwards, meanwhile, declared personal bankruptcy in 1992, announced that his next career would be as a lawyer (a dream he never fulfilled), and took some small consolation from the fact that if he had been born sixty years earlier, and had competed at the 1924 Winter Games in Chamonix, France, his Calgary jumps would have been good enough to win him Olympic gold.

Gretzky Goes to Hollywood—August 1988

Wayne Gretzky, with Los Angeles Kings owner
Bruce McNall (left), tries on the Kings' jersey for the
first time: "I wasn't going to let anyone tell me
where I would be playing."

WHEN THE EDMONTON Oilers announced the sale of their star player, Wayne Gretzky, to the Los Angeles Kings for the sum of US$15 million, the shock waves reverberated across Canada. "The best hockey player in the world was ours, and the Americans flew up from Hollywood in their private jet and bought him," lamented Vancouver sports columnist Jim Taylor in *Sports Illustrated* magazine.

The "trade of the century," as the media quickly dubbed it, came on 9 August 1988, at the end of a golden spring and summer for the twenty-seven-year-old hockey player. In May 1988, Gretzky had led the Oilers to their fourth Stanley Cup in five years. On 16 July, he had married Janet Jones, a rising Hollywood film actress, in what the media called Canada's "royal wedding." A six-page cover story in *Maclean's* magazine described the marriage as "the union of a talented and gentlemanly sports hero who, for many Canadians, embodies some of the nation's most cherished values, and his glamorous American princess." The couple planned to live in Edmonton, and Gretzky was looking forward to perhaps winning a few more Stanley Cups with the Oilers. But the team's owner, Edmonton businessman Peter Pocklington, had other plans in store for his prize asset.

By 1988, Gretzy had been with the Oilers for nine of his ten years as a hockey professional. A precocious talent, he first attracted national media attention as a novice at age eleven when he scored 378 goals in a single season for a team in his home town of Brantford, Ontario. Over the next six years, Gretzky shone as a junior player, competing internationally, setting records, winning awards, and attracting the attention of professional scouts from both the National Hockey League and the now-defunct World Hockey Association. He turned professional at age seventeen when Vancouver entrepreneur Nelson Skalbania, owner of the WHA's Indianapolis Racers, signed him to a four-year contract valued at $825,000. The following year, 1979, Skalbania traded Gretzky to the Edmonton Oilers, who were then in the WHA but soon to join the NHL. "I'm losing $40,000 a game," explained Skalbania. "I've got to move you."

Pocklington bought Gretzky sight unseen, primarily as a business proposition. "I remember thinking, here's this skinny little kid with peach fuzz and I thought, 'My God, I paid $750,000 for that?'" commented Pocklington. A self-made millionaire who made his fortune in land development, oil, meat-packing, and automobile dealerships, Pocklington—in Gretzky's estimation—knew little about professional hockey. But he did know about high-stakes gambling, and Gretzky—despite his failure to catch fire in Indianapolis— seemed like a potential winner. In January 1979, Pocklington signed the eighteen-year-old hockey player to a ten-year contract worth $3 million, with options for a further ten years. Gretzky soon provided Pocklington with a good return on his long-term investment. In his first NHL season with the Oilers, Gretzky tied for the league scoring title, won both the Hart Memorial Trophy for most valuable player and the Lady Byng Trophy for "sportsmanship and gentlemanly con- duct," and was also named to the NHL all-star team.

Between 1979 and 1988, the player the fans came to call "The Great One" dominated his sport as few athletes ever have. As the NHL's leading goal scorer for seven consecutive years, Gretzky broke several points-scoring records—including a still unmatched 215-point season in 1985–86—and led the Oilers to four Stanley Cup victories. However, the strain of playing high-pressure hockey during the regu- lar season and the playoffs, along with the toll associated with play- ing in exhibition games and all-star games and representing his country in Canada Cup tournaments, eventually started to wear him down. He was also emotionally drained after trying throughout the 1986–87 season to negotiate a no-trade clause into his personal serv- ices contract with Pocklington. In May 1987, Gretzky told his parents he was physically and mentally exhausted and that he wanted to get out of hockey. "You'll feel better after the summer," his father, Walter Gretzky, assured him. "No," insisted Wayne. "I think this is it for me."

A knee injury kept Gretzky off the ice for sixteen games

during the 1987–88 season. But when he returned, he helped the Oilers win their fourth Stanley Cup and he was no longer talking about quitting. He hoped to sign one last contract with the Oilers that would take him through to retirement at age thirty-three or thirty-four. However, Pocklington did not offer to extend his contract. The owner needed money because his other business interests were failing and Gretzky's contract was a liquid asset that he could sell for US$15 million. Pocklington decided to trade his star player at top market value now, while Gretzky was in top condition, rather than take whatever he could get when Gretzky got older and his talents started to decline.

Gretzky claimed he didn't know anything about Pocklington's plan until after the Oilers won the Stanley Cup in May 1988. He was honeymooning with Janet in Los Angeles when Bruce McNall, owner of the Los Angeles Kings, phoned to say he had received permission to talk to him about a possible trade. Gretzky was annoyed not to have heard anything about this from the Oilers organization, but agreed to talk to McNall. "If I was going to be traded, I liked the idea of going to Los Angeles, where Janet could resume her career."

The announcement touched off a frenzy of anger and dismay among Oilers fans, thousands of whom called the organization's head office and radio phone-in shows to protest the trade. But at an emotional news conference in Edmonton, Gretzky said that the move to Los Angeles was his idea. "For the benefit of Wayne Gretzky, my new wife and our expected child in the new year, it would be beneficial for everyone involved to let me play with the Los Angeles Kings." He choked back the tears as he made the impromptu statement. Later, he said that while he did ask to be sent to Los Angeles, he did so only after he discovered that Pocklington had been shopping him around to NHL owners in Detroit, New York, and Vancouver. "I wasn't going to let anyone tell me where I would be playing," he said. "I had been pleasing people all my life, so now I decided to do what's best for Wayne Gretzky."

Many people blamed Gretzky's pregnant wife for the trade. They believed that Janet had forced Wayne to leave Canada so that she could resume her Hollywood career. One caller to an Edmonton radio show compared her to John Lennon's widow, Yoko Ono, whom

189

many Beatles fans blamed for the breakup of the group. Janet responded by phoning the *Edmonton Journal* and telling a reporter that the trade had nothing to do with her. "Owners don't make $15 million trades for wives," she said. "Peter Pocklington is the reason Wayne Gretzky is no longer an Edmonton Oiler."

Pocklington became the next target of blame for Oilers fans. Once hailed as an entrepreneurial hero for bringing an NHL franchise to Edmonton, the owner was now denounced as a scoundrel. Hockey fans hanged him in effigy outside Edmonton's Northlands Coliseum, where the Oilers played their home games, and threatened to boycott the meat and dairy products of the companies he owned. Pocklington retaliated by doing some name calling of his own. He characterized Gretzky as a "great actor" and accused his former favourite son of faking his anguish when he wept at the Edmonton news conference. "I thought he pulled it off beautifully when he showed how upset he was, but he wants the big dream," said Pocklington. "I call Los Angeles the land of the big trip, and he wants to go where the trips are the biggest." Gretzky angrily denied that he shed crocodile tears at the news conference and said he was genuinely sad to be leaving his friends on the Oilers team. "I had literally grown up with these guys, and the roots that I was cutting off were deep." He felt betrayed by Pocklington, and so did Edmontonians.

The Gretzky deal underlined the reality that professional hockey was a business and that the players were merely commodities, for sale to the highest bidder. The game might also be about entertainment and sporting achievement, but first and foremost it was about making money. Gretzky could have stayed in Edmonton, and the Oilers could have set a standard for winning championships that would have remained unsurpassed for another century. "But Peter Pocklington knew what he needed, and it wasn't more Stanley Cups," said Gretzky. "He didn't need to sell more tickets. His arena was already sold out. He needed cash." Pocklington made a business decision aimed at propping up his failing financial empire, and Gretzky made a business decision to take the money and run. The Kings started him at US $2 million a year, base salary, plus thousands more for special appearances.

While Gretzky did make hockey a success in Hollywood, and

helped move the Kings from eighteenth place to fourth place in the NHL during his first season with the team, he again found himself dealing with an owner whose financial empire was in the process of crumbling. Bruce McNall eventually ran out of money, and was later convicted of fraud and sent to jail for five years. Subsequent Kings owners had money problems too, and Gretzky finally grew tired of the corporate instability that undercut the quality of the team. In 1996, he asked for a trade and was sent to the St. Louis Blues. Later that year, he moved to the New York Rangers.

With advancing age, and without much of a supporting cast, the thirty-five-year-old Gretzky performed poorly as a so-called "Broadway Blueshirt." After three lack-lustre seasons with the Rangers, he decided to cut the drama short before people started to walk out of the theatre. In April 1999, he finally called it quits and announced his retirement from hockey. Doubting he could play at an acceptable level for another season, and not wanting to drop his standards, he decided to quit. Gretzky had always said that he felt an obligation to play his best hockey every day because some young fan in the stands might be seeing him for the first time.

Gretzky continued to live in the United States, where he had extensive business interests, after his retirement. Canada's loss would remain America's (and Gretzky's) gain. However, in March 2002, Gretzky had Canadians cheering again from coast to coast when the team of hockey players he picked to play for Canada in the Salt Lake City Olympics defeated the Americans and brought home the gold. For one brief shining moment it was as if Gretzky had never left. Canada's one-time national sporting hero had returned to the nation's television screens to show that his sport didn't always have to be about American big bucks. It could also be about a group of talented players playing for nothing more than national pride.

Alberta Acquires Unusual
Art Legacy—1991

THE ALBERTA ART Foundation, now replaced by the Alberta Foundation for the Arts, was a provincial government agency established to support and contribute to the development of the visual arts in Alberta. In 1972, it organized an art collection with the idea of preserving and showcasing the work of the province's best artists. Yet, when foundation administrator Wai Tin Ng had the opportunity to acquire the paintings of an obscure British Columbia artist named Sveva Caetani, he was happy to make an exception and include a non-Albertan in the collection. In the process he drew attention to one of the more unusual stories in the history of Canadian art.

Sveva Ersilia Giovanella Maria Caetani di Sermoneta was a painter of sombre allegorical watercolours whose life story could have inspired a novel by Henry James. She was born into one of Rome's oldest aristocratic families, with records dating back to the tenth century when Pope Gelasio II (a Caetani) held office. The family's position in the history of the papacy was further entrenched in 1294 with the election of Cardinal Benedetto Caetani as Pope Boniface VIII. The family was later influential in promoting the unification of Italy, and numbered among its members various scientists, scholars, statesmen, and literary figures, including Sveva's great-grandfather Michelangelo Caetani, who published essays on Dante Alighieri's classic, *The Divine Comedy*.

Sveva's father, the Duke of Sermoneta, was the author of an

influential twelve-volume work on Islam and served as a deputy in the Italian parliament. In 1901, he married a member of the Colonna family, who were centuries-old enemies of the Caetani. That marriage dissolved before Sveva was born. Her mother was the duke's second wife, the former Ofelia Fabiani, daughter of a prominent Roman civil engineer.

In 1921, when Sveva was four, the duke moved his family to Canada, where he had hunted bear as a young man and now wanted to become a fruit farmer. With Fascism gaining political ground, Italy had lost its appeal for him. While he continued to stay in touch with his political allies and returned to Italy several times, Caetani eventually had a falling out with Mussolini, who took away his Italian citizenship.

The family, accompanied by a Danish-born secretary known as Miss Jüül, settled in the Okanagan Valley town of Vernon, British Columbia. The duke bought an orchard with a Victorian-style mansion on the grounds, and revelled in his new role as gentleman farmer. Sveva was educated first at home by English governesses, and then at Crofton House, a private boarding school for girls in Vancouver. She read, spoke, and wrote in English, French, and Italian, and made frequent trips with her family to Europe, where she had private instruction in painting and drawing.

At Crofton House, Sveva made friends for the first time, something she had never been allowed to do while being educated at home in Vernon. But her gradually expanding world suddenly collapsed in 1935 when her father died of cancer. Her mother, Ofelia, who had never adjusted to life in Canada, spoke little English, and had few Canadian friends, became a recluse. She forced Sveva, then a strikingly beautiful eighteen-year-old, to share her isolation. "If you leave me, I shall die," said Ofelia, claiming to suffer from a heart condition. She bullied her daughter into cutting herself off from the outside world and even insisted that the two of them share a bedroom until Sveva rebelled by moving her bed onto a landing.

Sveva lived like this for the next twenty-five years. Her despotic mother granted her permission to order books from around the world and to read widely, but refused to let her write or paint. Letters from her school friends and relatives had to be screened by

Ofelia before Sveva could read them. A high fence enclosed the property and four Great Pyrenees dogs stood guard to keep intruders and strangers out. All visitors, aside from tradesmen, were turned away.

Ofelia Caetani died in 1960 and virtually disinherited her daughter by leaving the bulk of her fortune to the Roman Catholic Church. Sveva, at age forty-three, had to find a way of earning a living in order to survive. She learned to drive, joined various local clubs and associations, and, without any formal training, taught European history, French, art, and social studies at a local parochial school. She later earned a teaching certificate from the University of Victoria and, with the encouragement of an art teacher named John Cawood, resumed the painting she had abandoned in 1935. In 1975, she returned to Vernon, moved back into the family mansion after Miss Jüül died, and taught at a local high school.

In 1978, eighteen years after her mother's death, Sveva started to exorcise her experience through a series of fifty-six watercolour paintings inspired by Dante's *Divine Comedy*. These ethereally powerful paintings, which she titled *Recapitulation*, were dedicated to her "adored" father and reflected scenes from her family's life set amid metaphysical images of hell, purgatory, and heaven. The paintings were accompanied by poetry, prose, and pen-and-ink depictions of allegorical symbols drawn from different religions.

The paintings, some of which were 2.5 metres tall, demonstrated not only a highly developed sense of design but a luminous quality that, Sveva said, came from a richly layered brush technique favoured by the Mughal dynasty painters of seventeenth-century India. In 1986, Sveva showed some of the paintings at a solo exhibition in Grande Prairie, Alberta, and subsequently at solo and group shows in Edmonton, Ottawa, Toronto, and Vancouver.

Sveva retired from teaching in 1983 because of knee problems that eventually consigned her to a wheelchair. She continued to paint with hands stiffened by arthritis. Although there was a tragic tone to both her words and her images, neither bitterness nor rancour were directed toward the mother who had crushed and consumed her youth and promise. Ofelia appeared in the paintings explained and forgiven as the mother "who without effort could transmit the unknowable." Her father appeared as her guide and mentor, playing the poet Virgil ("my master and my author") to Sveva's Dante, "whose yearning for the immeasurable I have inherited."

The paintings took Sveva eleven years to complete, by which time "my hands and fingers were barely co-operating." When her arthritic hands eventually prevented her from holding a brush or a pen, she continued to work on the accompanying text with a computer. "Being born," she wrote, "is like being fished out of nameless waters and landed on an alien deck, consigned to an alien fate, handled by ignorant strangers, and eaten once the flapping is stilled."

Neither the British Columbia nor the Canadian art establishments were particularly impressed by Sveva's work, which despite its origin had clear affinities with the sophisticated horror-comic art of New York and Los Angeles. One Vancouver critic described it as "curious art, metaphysical, fantastical and entirely outside the stream of contemporary theory and practice." However, Sveva was determined to find a home for her "children," as she called the paintings, and was pleased when the Alberta Art Foundation finally agreed to accept them in 1991.

Sveva died in 1994 at age seventy-six. By that time, her *Recapitulation* series had been borrowed for exhibition purposes by many of Alberta's public galleries and government departments. "Thousands of people have viewed these magnificent watercolours and have written to us expressing their admiration," said foundation chairman Richard Jarvis. He expressed great relief that the paintings, which were stored in the basement vault of the foundation's Beaver House gallery in Edmonton, escaped without damage in October 1994, when a water pipe burst, flooding the basement.

Sveva bequeathed her one-hundred-year-old family home to the city of Vernon to be turned into an arts centre. It stands in modest contrast to the Renaissance Cachigi Palace on the Tiber, which houses the Caetani Foundation for Islamic Studies that her father founded shortly before moving to Canada in 1921. But, even Henry James might have agreed that the Vernon house and the Alberta art collection have combined as a fitting monument to the last of the Caetani di Sermoneta.

AIDS Virus as Assault
Weapon—May 1995

THE STORY FIRST hit the front pages in February 1993, when Con Boland, a flamboyant Edmonton portrait photographer, told police that an "unknown assailant" came to his front door and threw sulphuric acid at his face, burning his neck, shoulders, and chest. Four people were subsequently charged with a series of offences, including conspiracy to murder Boland. They were his former lover Marilyn Tan, her new lover Geoffrey Clarkson, and two private detectives hired by Clarkson to implicate Boland in alleged narcotics activity. The charges against the three men were soon dropped, primarily because of tainted wiretap evidence. But some of the charges against Tan stuck and, by the time she went to trial in May 1995, her case had taken on the sleazy dimensions of a TV trash talk show. "Edmonton's trial of the century," pronounced the Edmonton-based *Western Report* magazine. "High society characters and tales of explicit sex highlight the case against Marilyn Tan."

The acid attack, as it turned out, was not the only assault Tan was accused of committing on Boland. Eight months earlier, in June 1992, she had allegedly injected him with HIV-positive blood while they were having sex in a California hotel room. It was mainly because of this incident that she went to trial in Edmonton in 1995, on charges of aggravated assault, conspiracy to administer a "noxious substance" (the AIDS virus), and twice administering the substance. She thus became the first person in North America to be charged with using the virus as a weapon. Additionally she was charged with uttering a death threat against Jeanette Kunkel, the woman who became Boland's new sex partner after he left Tan.

The case spotlighted the sordid end of a relationship that began in 1984 when Tan arrived at Boland's doorstep, responding to his ad for a receptionist. He was then a boyish-looking thirty-six-year-old establishing a reputation for himself as "photographer to the stars," with a roster of high-profile clients that included hockey great Wayne Gretzky, Pierre Trudeau, Peter Lougheed, and Edmonton Oilers owner Peter Pocklington. She was a dark-haired twenty-four-year-old beauty, divorced with a four-year-old son, and had been living in Edmonton for about two years. Born in the Philippines and raised in poverty, Tan had immigrated to Canada at age seventeen with her mother and an older brother, married at age twenty, had a baby boy whom she nicknamed Tex, and then divorced.

Tan had fifty dollars in her purse when she and Tex arrived in Edmonton from Winnipeg. She found a low-rent apartment, worked behind the counter at a 7-Eleven store, sold clothing at a women's fashion store, and then went on the road as a band singer. She didn't have much of a voice but, according to the agent who booked her, "she had a real artistic sense and she could work an audience."

She applied for Boland's receptionist job in order to get off the road. But her qualifications failed to impress him. She couldn't type and she knew nothing about photography. Plus she had a "foreign" accent, and Boland thought that would be a turnoff for potential customers. But he did like her smile and, though he hired someone else to answer his phone and do his paperwork, he found another place in his life for Tan. He phoned her later that day and invited her out for dinner. "She was vivacious," he said. "She had some kind of charisma."

They saw one another regularly over the next year, and intermittently in the years after that, when she worked for a time as his live-in sales assistant. She continued to sing and Boland occasionally went to see her when she performed in Edmonton. A musician who played both piano and guitar, Boland could see that Tan had little musical talent. But she "had really good stage presence. The way she moved was a pleasure to watch."

Boland, like Tan, was also an immigrant who came to Canada seeking a better life. Born in the Netherlands, he arrived as a nineteen-year-old in 1967, when the Canadian government was offering interest-free loans to foreign nationals to buy one-way airline tickets to Canada and become landed immigrants. After working in an Edmonton photo lab for a couple of years, he opened his own studio in a house that he bought in the inner-city community of Riverdale, and hung out his shingle as a portrait photographer.

In 1970, Boland married an Edmonton schoolteacher named Diana Tkachuk. It was an "open" marriage that lasted about six years. He slept with other women and she took a lover who, for a while, actually lived with the couple in their Riverdale home. After Tkachuk left him in 1976, Boland began consorting with prostitutes and contracted a series of sexually transmitted diseases. He also dabbled in recreational drugs but his partying didn't seem to adversely affect his photography business, which grew and flourished. He added rooms and a sauna to his three-storey studio, entertained lavishly, turned his yard into an award-winning show garden, and drove expensive cars.

Boland continued to associate with prostitutes after he began dating Tan. They argued about this at first but, said Boland, she eventually came to accept him for what he was—a philanderer with a taste for rough trade and sadomasochistic sex. She agreed to watch him while he had sex with other women and she willingly indulged his fetishes and fantasies when he introduced her to some "light s & m."

But while Tan may have been prepared to temporarily share Boland with others and participate in kinky sex to keep him happy, her long-term goal was to acquire wealth, respect, stability, and marriage. Boland began paying her a salary to book portrait appointments and do promotions for him, and he also provided a home in his studio for Tan and her son. But, in her estimation, he never gave her enough to cover her clothing, restaurant, and phone bills, and she was frustrated by his refusal to consider the possibility of turning their informal live-in arrangement into something more legally binding. He told her he had already given half his assets to his ex-wife and he wasn't about to go down that road again.

The relationship eventually foundered on the rocks of Tan's lavish spending habits and Boland's lack of commitment. Tan moved out and settled in an apartment downtown. After a year, she moved back and attempted reconciliation, but discovered that nothing had really changed. Boland was determined to continue seeing other women and Tan had to accept the possibility that they might never marry. She continued, however, to work for him and live in his studio.

During the early 1990s, Tan struck up a friendship with Rachel Deitch, a sophisticated socialite who came to have her portrait done by Boland. Deitch was about to divorce her husband, and she and Tan enrolled in a Arthur Murray dance course "so we could meet wealthy men." But Tan couldn't stop thinking of Boland. Even though she and Tex now lived by themselves in the studio while Boland lived in a small house across the street, she couldn't put the relationship behind her. She began plotting revenge after she discovered Boland was seeing a younger woman named Jeanette Kunkel. "What would you do if you wanted to hurt someone?" Tan asked Deitch. "I'd inject them with a virus," replied Deitch. Tan agreed: "Injecting someone with the AIDS virus is a good idea." Deitch, who subsequently became the prosecution's leading witness, testified that she and Tan also discussed throwing acid in Boland's face "so he wouldn't be able to take pictures any more and so that nobody would want him."

Deitch testified that Tan acquired a vial of HIV-tainted blood from Tan's older sister Evelyn—a nurse who worked with AIDS patients in Los Angeles—and that Tan first injected Boland with the contaminated blood during a violent love-making session at Boland's studio in April 1992. However, Tan "wasn't sure if she had got enough of the virus into Con, and so she would have to do it again." Tan arranged for a second tryst ("for old time's sake") at a Long Beach hotel in June 1992, and that's when she allegedly gave Boland enough of the virus for him to subsequently test HIV positive.

On 11 June 1992, the day before Tan was due to fly to California for her "one last fling" with Boland, she and Deitch drove to Whyte Avenue in Edmonton's Old Strathcona shopping district to visit Boland's new lover, Jeanette Kunkel. Deitch went into the bead shop where Kunkel was working, said something about her car having a problem, and asked Kunkel to accompany her out into the parking lot. When they got there, Tan—who was wearing sunglasses and a black leather raincoat—jumped out of the car, slammed Kunkel up against a wall, and threatened to have her killed if she didn't stop seeing Boland. The experience scared Kunkel so much that she fled to Vancouver and hid there for two weeks. When she returned she told Boland she did not wish to see him again.

Deitch's description of the California assignation, as told to her by Tan, provided the media with plenty of fodder for voyeuristic stories about bondage, whips, blindfolds, and the other paraphernalia of sadomasochistic sex. However, Boland testified that he could remember little about the four-day rendezvous beyond the fact that they took a room at the Holiday Inn in Long Beach, and that he was surprised to find Tan's sister Evelyn staying in an adjoining room. He did remember that he drank alcohol in his room and that Tan had dominated him in bed: "I would lose control and I would be her puppy." Then he passed out. He awoke the next morning to find a large bruise on his left thigh.

Tan moved out of Boland's studio a few months after they returned to Edmonton from California. Her quest to find "wealthy men" had paid dividends, and she was ready to move on to someone new. One conquest was Bruce Sansom, a married fifty-six-year-old Edmonton investment manager whose clients included the Edmonton Oilers and Procter & Gamble. She was also interested in Geoffrey Clarkson, a fifty-eight-year-old New Zealand rancher and software merchant who did a lot of business in Alberta, buying frozen cattle embryos. He was divorced and looking for a companion.

Tan described Sansom as her "fairy godfather" and said he offered her an "investment opportunity" that supposedly would be worth $2 million at the end of ten years. But he fell by the wayside when Clarkson arrived in Edmonton and offered Tan $1 million to become his permanent travelling companion. She turned that offer down, saying she wanted to stay in Edmonton and get into the photography business. He responded by loaning her $1 million, which she used to buy six Edmonton photo studios. Boland testified that she also tried to buy his studio but he refused her offer.

Clarkson bought a $535,000 house for Tan in Glenora, one of

Edmonton's most exclusive residential districts, and Tan arranged for a $195,000 renovation job prior to moving in. Court documents showed that Clarkson also gave Tan two cars valued at a total of $87,000 and jewellery worth $130,000. Not content with that, Tan launched a "palimony" suit against Boland, claiming a share of his business and assets. This did not sit well with Deitch who now saw Tan as being little more than a grasping opportunist and thought that Boland should be warned.

Boland took an HIV test after Deitch told him the full story of what she understood had happened in the California hotel room. When he tested positive, in December 1992, he went to the police. They listened to his story with interest but saw no reason to pursue the matter at that time. It was only after Boland was attacked with acid, two months later, that police decided to take action. They obtained authorization to tap the telephones of people they suspected might be involved in the acid attack. One of these was Russell Forsythe, an Edmonton private investigator employed by Clarkson.

In July 1993, police charged Clarkson, Tan, Forsythe, and Forsythe's assistant, Walter Peel. Among the charges laid were conspiracy to murder Boland and Deitch, conspiracy to plant narcotics on Boland and Deitch, and unlawfully wounding, maiming, disfiguring, or endangering Boland. However, the paperwork that authorized the wiretaps was flawed, and the charges against the three men were stayed and eventually dropped for lack of admissible evidence. Only Tan remained accused, in connection with the alleged HIV attack on Boland and the death threat uttered against Kunkel.

The trial began on 1 May 1995, and attracted international attention from media in New Zealand, Hong Kong, New York, Los Angeles, London, and Switzerland. Tan, then thirty-five, was the first person in North America to be charged with injecting someone with HIV-tainted blood. Local media characterized it as "the biggest thing" to hit Edmonton since the July 1988 wedding of Wayne Gretzky and Janet Jones. It topped the local news day after day and consigned the other two big trials of that time—the O. J. Simpson case in Los Angeles and the Paul Bernardo-Karla Homolka trial in Ontario—to the inside pages of the newspapers. An Alberta publisher suggested

BOONDOGGLES, BONANZAS, AND OTHER ALBERTA STORIES

the Tan story could result in a bestselling book and perhaps a top-rated TV movie because "the details of the case are so bizarre that it's difficult to believe they weren't invented by Hollywood." It was all heady stuff for a city more used to stories about hockey, curling and provincial politics. An Edmonton radio station held a contest asking listeners to guess the prices of sex toys used by Boland and Tan, and the Gone On Safari Café in Old Strathcona offered a "Marilyn Tan Scramble" on its breakfast menu. For $5.50 the customer would get "three fresh eggs, beaten and whipped, injected with some spice, cluttered with vegetables and laid out on a platter with million-dollar accompaniments."

The key witnesses for the Crown were Boland and Deitch. Also testifying were Kunkel and Bruce Sansom, who fought unsuccessfully to keep his identity secret because he wanted to protect his wife and four children and didn't want his name associated with the "smutty and dirty" facts of the case. In his testimony, this so-called "fairy godfather" said Boland tried to blackmail him into persuading Tan to drop her palimony lawsuit, and that he threatened to take a box of incriminating photos and letters to the media if Sansom didn't co-operate.

Boland testified that he went to California with Tan because he wanted to end their relationship on good terms. She brought along the sexual props and "promised some really wild love-making." He said that during the months leading up to the California trip he had sex only a few times with Tan and once with Kunkel, and never saw prostitutes. However, he did admit under cross-examination to having sex with prostitutes during the years before and since, and acknowledged that he took drugs with prostitutes, using hypodermic syringes that they supplied. Boland also conceded that the bruise on his thigh in California might have come from Tan's whipping rather than from the needle with which she allegedly injected him.

Much of the Crown's case hinged on the testimony of Deitch, who said she was frightened initially to come forward with what she knew about the 1992 plot against Boland because she believed Tan's sister would kill her. She was placed under round-the-clock police protection after she revealed the plot to Boland.

Tan's lawyer, Sterling Sanderman, didn't call any witnesses

and based his defence on his contention that neither Boland nor Deitch could be believed. The lawyer took particular aim at Boland, saying he could easily have become infected with HIV during his encounters with drug-carrying prostitutes. Mr. Justice Keith Ritter agreed. "Mr. Boland's testimony takes me in circles," he said. Given that Boland had an admitted fondness for picking up prostitutes, said Ritter, "I simply cannot believe that Mr. Boland lived a life of near celibacy in the calendar year of 1992." The fact that the photographer had admitted to shooting up drugs with hookers and had contracted several other sexually transmitted diseases over the years, further undermined the Crown's assertion that the alleged injection infected Boland. "Mr. Boland lived in a fashion that placed him at significant risk of catching HIV," said Ritter. "He is not a trustworthy witness."

Ritter was less dismissive of Deitch's testimony. But because she was an unindicted co-conspirator in the alleged crime, Ritter said the Crown needed more corroborating forensic evidence to back up her claims. Referring to the ongoing O. J. Simpson murder trial, the judge said, "I don't have any blood-soaked socks or gloves in this case." He acquitted Tan of injecting Boland with the HIV virus, but found her guilty of uttering death threats against Kunkel and sentenced her to three months in jail.

Much of the talk about bestselling books and TV movies evaporated when Tan was acquitted on the AIDS-related charges. "It's going to be yesterday's news by the time it comes out," said one publisher. "Come to think of it, it's already yesterday's news." The only one to actually write a book about the case was Boland himself whose self-published monograph, *Beneath the Surface: My True Story*, appeared briefly on the shelves in 1997 and quickly disappeared.

Boland continued to maintain a high profile in Edmonton after the trial, telling interviewers that the experience had helped turn him into a "very positive person who loves gardening and flowers and creating music." By the beginning of 2000, his studio work had expanded from portrait photography into digital imaging and website design, and he was billing himself as a European "master photographer."

The others in the case dropped out of sight. Deitch retreated to the solitude of her Edmonton bungalow and refused to talk any more about the case. Clarkson retired to Laguna Beach, California, after selling the Glenora house and calling his liens on the photo studios purchased by Tan. Sansom's wife divorced him in 1996. He moved to Tucson, Arizona, after selling his investment company to a Connecticut-based money management firm. Tan served her sentence and moved to Los Angeles where she tried unsuccessfully to sell her story to book publishers and film producers.

Compensation for Sterilization Victims —January 1996

❧

SHE WENT PUBLIC with her pain and won her battle for compensation. When Leilani Muir sought damages from the Alberta government for being involuntarily sterilized at age fourteen while wrongly confined to a provincially run mental institution, her case shone a light into a dark corner of the province's medical history.

Between 1928 and 1972, some twenty-eight hundred people in Alberta were forcibly sterilized in a human engineering experiment intended to prevent those considered "mentally defective" or "psychotic" from having children and passing on the "evil" of their disability. Native girls as young as thirteen, already-infertile Down Syndrome boys, children with cerebral palsy, illiterate immigrants from Eastern Europe, and delinquent youths from broken homes were among those sterilized.

The sterilizations were performed at Red Deer's Provincial Training School for Mental Defectives (later renamed the Michener Centre), an institution once considered progressive, humane, and well run. Ernest Manning, Social Credit premier of Alberta from 1943 to 1968, entrusted his eldest son, Keith, to the school for several years, and frequently visited him there.

Muir was admitted to the school in 1955 at age ten, when her alcoholic mother and stepfather abandoned her. Born to a father she never knew, and a mother who frequently beat and starved her, she spent a miserable childhood moving from one southern Alberta farm community to the next. Her teachers viewed her as a "problem child" because her hunger often drove her to stealing other children's lunches. Before being admitted to the Red Deer school she was tested by a Calgary psychiatrist who stated in a report that her problems "had an emotional involvement rather than a primary mental deficiency." However, she managed to achieve only a "sub-normal" score of sixty-four on an IQ test administered by the school doctor. (Her lawyer said later that the damage caused by her abusive upbringing contributed to the poor result.) That earned her the label of a "mental defective—moron" and put her on the road to sterilization. In 1957, without testing her again, the Red Deer school doctor recommended to the government that she be sterilized. Two years later, she was admitted to the school clinic, supposedly to have her appendix removed. It wasn't until years later, married and unable to become pregnant, that Muir learned her fallopian tubes had been removed.

Alberta's sterilization policy was the product of a once-popular but now long-discredited pseudo-science called eugenics. In vogue during the 1920s and 1930s, it held that mental illnesses —broadly defined to include everything from psychosis to drug addiction—were almost invariably inherited and that the only hope for an improvement in the quality of society's gene pool was through selective breeding. In Canada, eugenics supporters pushed sterilization into law in both Alberta and British Columbia; the law satisfied those who believed that radical measures were justified to protect their communities from social inefficiency and immorality. Sterilization laws were also passed in thirty-one American states. Efforts to pass sterilization laws in Quebec, Ontario, and Manitoba failed because provincial politicians anxious about the Catholic vote rallied to oppose what was, in fact, legalized surgical birth control.

Among the early Canadian supporters of eugenics were the inventor Alexander Graham Bell and the pioneering socialist Tommy Douglas, who wrote, "Those least fitted to propagate have done so, and have filled our jails and mental hospitals at an alarming rate." Douglas later abandoned eugenics, after being alarmed by what he saw during a wartime trip to Germany where thousands of mentally handicapped citizens were sterilized and then gassed in the service of Nazi master-race theories.

Alberta's eugenics campaigners included such feminist icons as Nellie McClung and Emily Murphy. Indeed, Murphy set aside her more celebrated legal battle to have Canadian women officially recognized as "persons" to tour Alberta in 1926 with fervent speeches about Canada needing "human thoroughbreds." "We protect the public against diseased and distempered cattle," she wrote in one of the many articles in which she used the pen name, Janey Canuck. "We should similarly protect them against the offal of humanity."

At first, the Alberta law, enacted by the United Farmers of Alberta government, required parental consent. Later on that was ruled unnecessary. Evidence in the Muir case showed that it was standard procedure for institutionalized boys, when they reached age twelve, to appear before the province's four-member Eugenics Board, which included a philosophy professor and two doctors. The boys were scheduled for vasectomies, and sometimes castrations, as little as a week later. In many instances, sterilization was a prerequisite for admission to the Red Deer training school. In other cases, refusal to comply meant indefinite detention. One woman said she spent more than fifty years inside rather than submit to an operation.

Muir lived in the institution until 1965, when she was twenty. Then, she lived with her mother for a while, and eventually settled by herself in Victoria, British Columbia, where she worked as a waitress at a department store café. She married and divorced twice. She said her second marriage fell apart after she and her husband were denied adoption.

In 1972, the Alberta government finally repealed the Sexual Sterilization Act. The Conservative premier, Peter Lougheed, said he was shocked to discover it was still on the books. It was not listed in the general index of operating laws and the government only became aware of it when an Edmonton gynecologist, James Goodwin, publicly denounced the act as "reminiscent of the sterilization laws of Nazi Germany." Goodwin charged that sterilizations were still being performed in Alberta on the basis of "very sketchy evidence" of mental disability. The government responded that involuntary sterilizations had not been performed for several years, but agreed that the law should be struck from the books. "We thought it was a pretty reprehensible piece of legislation," said MLA Dave King. "We had to get it off the books, because we had to be sure it would not sit awaiting use for wrong political reasons."

Muir began seeking legal action in British Columbia in 1989, when she was forty-four. She said she wanted an apology from the Alberta government and $2.5 million in general and punitive damages for being wrongfully admitted to the Red Deer training school, and for being wrongfully sterilized and inadequately educated. A psychiatric test administered in Victoria and a second test administered in Edmonton showed her to be of low-normal intelligence.

The case opened in an Edmonton courtroom in June 1995. A government lawyer admitted that Muir was wrongly sterilized and thus entitled to general damages, but rejected the claim that she was wrongly admitted to the training school or wasn't properly educated there. Muir told the court about her anguished and ultimately unsuccessful efforts to reverse the procedure, and said she longed for children "more than anything in the world." "Nobody has the right to play God with other people's lives—nobody," she said, tears streaming down her cheeks.

The most damaging testimony in the case came from an Edmonton law professor, Gerald Robertson, who reviewed Eugenics Board minutes and patient files and said that the board often broke its own rules, rushing through approvals in assembly-line style. By the early 1940s, patients were being approved for sterilization in five minutes or less, and the board was largely relying on other people for recommendations. Many people were sterilized because they had behavioural problems, not mental disabilities.

How could a civilized society have allowed this to happen? Muir's lawyer, Jon Faulds, concluded that the eugenics movement capitalized on a general sense of public unease about such problems as unemployment, crime, and immigration. "And it offered a very simple solution in this slogan: Sterilize the Unfit."

The government offered to pay $60,000 to compensate Muir, but she dismissed the offer as inadequate and continued to press her suit. Her persistence paid off. On 26 January 1996, seven years after she first sought legal action, a Court of Queen's Bench judge finally awarded her $740,780 in compensation, plus $230,000 in legal costs, for wrongful sterilization, confinement, pain, and suffering. "The Eugenics Board treated people like guinea pigs and failed to follow the law," said Justice Joanne Veit. "It changed, warped and haunted her life." Muir said she planned to quit her job, buy a house, and travel the world to tell her story.

The government did not appeal the ruling. Nor would it apologize to Muir. The provincial justice minister, Brian Evans, said the Conservatives shouldn't be expected to apologize for something that happened in 1959 when Social Credit was in power. "She got all she is going to get," he said. "We dealt with her in what we feel was a very reasonable manner."

Publicity about the Muir case encouraged hundreds of others to seek legal action. The government said it would oppose a class action suit and would deal separately with each individual. Government lawyer Doug Black said the government's argument would be based on the fact that the eugenics policy was consistent with the mores of the time. "The government provided for many of these individuals the only stable, loving environment they ever encountered," he said.

Close to nine hundred people filed claims through thirty-eight law firms, most seeking a straight $1 million in compensation. The government first responded by invoking a rarely used legal procedure—the override clause in the Canadian constitution—to limit any court damages to a maximum of $150,000 per individual. However, in 1998, the government settled out of court with two omnibus compensation packages which included legal costs and amounted to a total of $150 million. Individual settlements were not disclosed, but newspaper reports said they ranged from $200,000 to $800,000. Additionally, the provincial justice minister, David Hancock, finally offered an apology to the victims on behalf of the province. "This should never have happened in Alberta's history," he said. "And God help us, it should never, ever happen again."

Muir remained in Alberta after her case was concluded, married again, and announced, in February 2001, that she would run for the New Democrats in Leduc in the 12 March provincial election. Her main goal, she said, was to oppose Premier Ralph

Klein's *Bill 11*, which proposed to allow private medical clinics to keep patients overnight. She came third in the race behind Liberal Joyce Assen and the winner, Conservative Albert Klapstein. The contentious *Bill 11*, which Muir had hoped to oppose, was passed in May 2002 and four months later, the government used the provisions of the new act to allow a private clinic in Calgary to perform surgeries requiring overnight stays.

Afterword

MY THANKS TO the following authors for writing the books that supported my storytelling in *Boondoggles, Bonanzas, and Other Alberta Stories:*

Paul Emile Breton for *The Big Chief of the Prairies: The Life of Father Lacombe;* Sveva Caetani for *Recapitulation: A Journey;* Rod Campbell for *Playing the Field: The Story of the Edmonton Folk Music Festival;* William E. Code for *The Code Inquiry: Final Report of the Inspector;* William James Cousins for *A History of the Crowsnest Pass;* Frank Dabbs for *Ralph Klein: A Maverick Life;* Hugh A. Dempsey for *Calgary: Spirit of the West;* Michael ("Eddie the Eagle") Edwards for *Eddie the Eagle: My Story;* Frank H. Ellis for *Canada's Flying Heritage;* David Finch and Gordon Jaremko for *Fields of Fire: An Illustrated History of Canadian Petroleum;* Barry Glen Ferguson for *Athabasca Oil Sands: Northern Resource Exploration, 1875–1951;* Lorne W. Gold for *The Canadian Habbakuk Project;* Ed Gould for *All Hell for a Basement: Medicine Hat, 1883–1983;* Katherine Govier for *Between Men;* Walter Gretzky and Jim Taylor for *Gretzky;* Wayne Gretzky and Rick Reilly for *Gretzky: An Autobiography;* Chris Gudgeon for *An Unfinished Conversation: The Life and Music of Stan Rogers;* Harry P. Harrison for *Culture Under Canvas: The Story of Tent Chautauqua;* Katherine Hughes for *Father Lacombe: The Black-Robe Voyageur;* Bea Hunter for *Last Chance Well: Legends & Legacies of Leduc No. 1;* Sheilagh S. Jameson for *Chautauqua in Canada;* Aubrey Kerr for *Leduc;* Graham A. MacDonald for *Where the Mountains Meet the Prairies: A History of Waterton Country;* Grant MacEwan for *The Sodbusters;* James G. MacGregor for *Father Lacombe;* Peter McKenzie-Brown, Gordon Jaremko and David Finch for *The Great Oil Age;* George de Mille for *Oil in Canada West: The Early Years;* Josephine

Phelan for *The Bold Heart: The Story of Father Lacombe*; Andrew Podnieks for *The Great One: The Life and Times of Wayne Gretzky*; Gerry Redmond for *Wayne Gretzky: The Great One*; Dan Riley, Hugh Dempsey, and Tom Primrose for *The Lost Lemon Mine: The Great Mystery of the Canadian Rockies*; William Rodney for *Kootenai Brown: Canada's Unknown Frontiersman*; Hazel B. Roen for *The Grass Roots of Dorothy*; Chic Scott for *Pushing the Limits: The Story of Canadian Mountaineering*; Charles Allen Seager for *A Proletariat in Wild Rose Country: The Alberta Coal Miners, 1905–1945*; Allan Shute and Margaret Fortier for *Riverdale: From Fraser Flats to Edmonton Oasis*; Wendy Smith for *Pay Yourself First: Donald Cormie and the Collapse of the Principal Group of Companies*; Clark C. Spence for *The Rainmakers: American Pluviculture to World War II*; Ron Stewart for *Goldrush: The Search for the Lost Lemon Mine*.

Index

A

B

C

U

Underwood, John, Elmer and George,
35–39
United Agricultural Association, 63,
67, 68
United Farmers of Alberta, 207
United Mine Workers of America, 75,
76, 79

V

Van Horne, William, 14
Vernon, B.C., 193–95
Vogel, Erik, 151, 152, 153

W

Wapiti Aviation, 150, 152, 153
Waterton Lakes, 22–27
Wetaskiwin, 58
Whalen, Don, 140, 142
Wickham, Terry, 142
Winnipeg, 42, 99, 100, 139, 142
Winnipeg Folk Festival, 139, 140
Wood, Henry Wise, 59
Wood, Sharon, 155–60
Wright, Wilbur and Orville, 36

Y

Yukon, 36, 66, 67

About Fifth House

FIFTH HOUSE PUBLISHERS, a Fitzhenry & Whiteside company, is a proudly western-Canadian press. Our publishing specialty is non-fiction as we believe that every community must possess a positive understanding of its worth and place if it is to remain vital and progressive. Fifth House is committed to "bringing the West to the rest" by publishing approximately twenty books a year about the land and people who make this region unique. Our books are selected for their quality, saleability, and contribution to the understanding of western-Canadian (and Canadian) history, culture, and environment.

Look for the following books by Brian Brennan in your local bookstore:

Alberta Originals: Stories of Albertans Who Made a Difference, $16.95*

Building a Province: 60 Alberta Lives, $14.95*

Scoundrels and Scallywags: Characters From Alberta's Past, $16.95*

* prices subject to change